WOODEN PUZZLES

The Best of SCROLLSAW
Woodworking & Crafts Magazine

WOODEN PUZZLES

31 Favorite Projects & Patterns

From the editors of
Scroll Saw Woodworking & Crafts

*Layered Marquetry Puzzles
by Steve Malavolta, page 74.*

FOX CHAPEL
PUBLISHING

© 2009 by Fox Chapel Publishing Company, Inc.

Wooden Puzzles: 31 Favorite Projects and Patterns is an original work, first published in 2009 by Fox Chapel Publishing Company, Inc. The patterns contained herein are copyrighted by the authors. Readers may make copies of these patterns for personal use. The patterns themselves, however, are not to be duplicated for resale or distribution under any circumstances. Any such copying is a violation of copyright law.

ISBN 978-1-56523-429-1

Publisher's Cataloging-in-Publication Data

Wooden puzzles : 31 favorite projects and patterns. -- 1st ed. -- East Petersburg, PA : Fox Chapel Publishing, c2009.

p. ; cm.

(The best of Scroll saw woodworking & crafts)

ISBN: 978-1-56523-429-1

Compiled by the editors of "Scroll saw woodworking & crafts."

1. Jigsaw puzzles--Patterns. 2. Jig saws-- Patterns.

3. Woodwork--Patterns. 4. Puzzles. I. Title. II. Series. III. Title: Scroll saw woodworking & crafts.

TT186. W66 2009
745.51/3--dc22   2009

To learn more about the other great books from Fox Chapel Publishing, or to find a retailer near you, call toll-free 800-457-9112 or visit us at *www.FoxChapelPublishing.com*.

Note to Authors: We are always looking for talented authors to write new books in our area of woodworking, design, and related crafts. Please send a brief letter describing your idea to Acquisition Editor, 1970 Broad Street, East Petersburg, PA 17520.

Printed in China
First printing: May 2009
Second printing: June 2010

Table of Contents

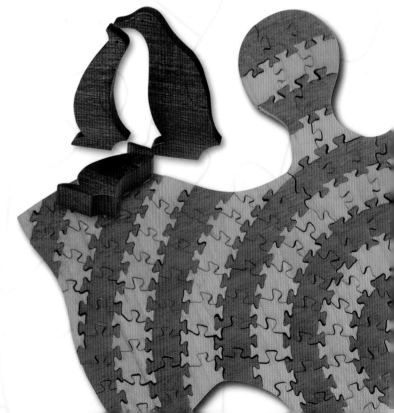

What You Can Make With This Book

Alpha-Snake Puzzle
Page 12

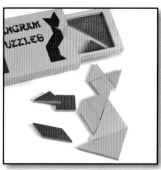

Pocket-Size Tangram Puzzle
Page 15

Create: The Word Game
Page 18

World's Most Difficult
Four-Piece Puzzle Page 21

Apple Alphabet Puzzle
Page 23

Paul Bunyan Tray Puzzle
Page 26

Dairy Delight Puzzle
Page 28

The Ultimate Puzzle
Page 31

Climbing Cats
Page 33

T-Rex Dinosaur Puzzle
Page 34

Ingenious Animal Family
Puzzles Page 36

Wizard Puzzle
Page 44

Star Puzzle
Page 46

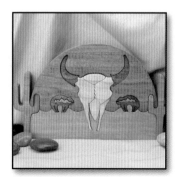

Southwestern Puzzle
Page 47

Teacher's Puzzle
Page 50

Noah's Ark Puzzle
Page 52

F-14 Swingwing Puzzle
Page 56

Woodimal® Lion
Page 60

Freestanding Animal Puzzles Page 62

Jonah and the Whale Puzzle Page 66

Woodimal® Moose
Page 68

Kangaroo Puzzle
Page 71

Layered Marquetry Puzzles
Page 74

Wooden Puzzle Vault
Page 82

Wooly Mammoth Puzzle
Page 88

Lateral Locking Lizard Puzzle Page 92

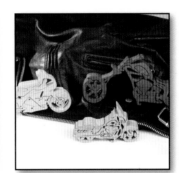

Motorcycle Puzzles
Page 96

Hidden Images Puzzle
Page 98

Elephant Woodimal®
Page 102

Owl Family Puzzle
Page 104

The Puzzle Art of Randy Crossman Page 106

Introduction

Scroll Saw Woodworking & Crafts magazine is proud to present this collection of some of our best puzzles for puzzle makers of all skill levels. Whether you enjoy painted projects, the look of natural wood, gifts for children, or puzzles that employ some woodworking techniques, you're bound to find just the right project in this book.

More than just a pattern book, however, the following pages also contain tips, techniques, and stories from many of our contributors that will hopefully inspire you to try both these puzzles and your own creations. For instance, master puzzle makers Steve Malavolta and Randy Crossman share their puzzles, tips, and stories, while Judy and Dave Peterson offer just what you need to create their simple but elegant designs.

The puzzles in this book are broken down into sections according to skill level—beginner puzzles, intermediate puzzles, and master puzzles—making it easy to find projects that suit you. This format also allows you to grow and challenge yourself as you become more comfortable and more skilled in puzzle making.

We hope this collection allows you to improve your skills and create beautiful puzzles to keep or to give as gifts.

Teacher's Puzzle by Judy and Dave Peterson, page 50.

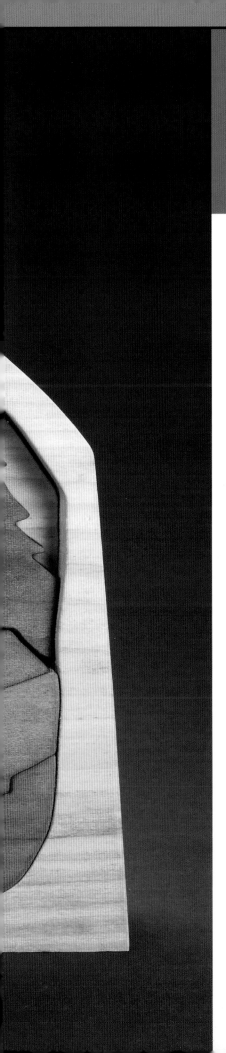

Beginner Puzzles

Though these puzzles are easy to make, you'll still end up with functional and attractive puzzles. Many of them make great gifts. All of the projects featured have the information you need to complete them. For some, that can include full step-by-step instructions; for others, all you'll need is simply the pattern, photo, and materials list.

Paul Bunyan Tray Puzzle by Russell Greenslade, page 26.

Alpha-Snake PUZZLE

Turn scrap wood into an ideal, enjoyable beginner's project

By John A. Nelson

Puzzles make great gifts for children. This one is particularly good for kids because it teaches them the alphabet—all 26 letters. As projects, puzzles are great for beginning scrollers because they allow you to practice cutting twists and turns, and they are forgiving. Once the pattern is removed, no one can tell if you strayed off the lines a little. Puzzle projects can also be a good way to use scrap wood—simply glue up material to size.

Before starting any puzzle, be sure the saw blade is exactly 90°, or square, to the table. If the blade is not square to the table, the pieces will not go together properly.

Step 1: Cut one piece of wood. Locate a piece of wood ¾" thick x 16" long x 9" wide. If you cannot find a piece of wood this size, simply glue up scrap wood to make the overall size.

Step 2: Sand the wood. Using medium-grit sandpaper, sand the top and bottom surfaces. Wipe the wood with a clean, damp cloth.

Step 3: Attach the pattern to the wood using temporary bond spray adhesive. Photocopy the pattern found on page 14. Be sure to spray only the pattern and not the wood.

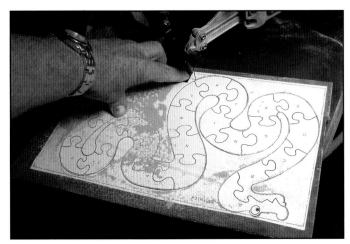

▲ **Step 4: Cut the snake's body.** Using a #5 skip-tooth blade, cut out the entire body. Try to keep the outside matting in place.

▲ **Step 5: Remove the snake's body.** Once the body is cut, remove it from the scrap wood and set the scrap wood aside for now.

▲ **Step 6: Cut the body in half.** Using a #2 regular-tooth blade, cut the body at a joint approximately in the middle so it will be easier to cut into the 26 pieces. By doing this, you will not have to swing a big piece of wood around.

Step 7: Cut the remaining pieces. Continue using the #2 blade to cut the remaining pieces. Try to keep within the lines, but if you stray a bit, it will not matter.

Step 8: Re-assemble the snake. As you cut out the pieces, re-assemble the snake back into the scrap board.

Step 9: Remove burrs. After all the pieces are cut out and placed back into the scrap board, sand the pieces with fine-grit sandpaper to remove any burrs.

▲ **Step 10: Turn the entire assembly over.** Using medium-grit sandpaper, sand the back. If there are any more burrs, remove the snake from the board and carefully sand the body.

Step 11: Remove all dust. Using turpentine or paint thinner on a clean cloth, wipe all pieces until each piece is dust-free.

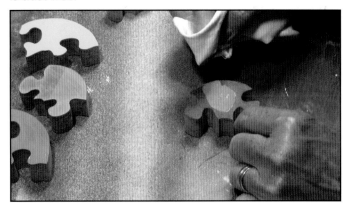

▲ **Step 12: Paint the pieces.** Using acrylic paint, choose the colors you would like for each piece of the puzzle. Start with the first color you have chosen and apply a tiny bit of paint to the top piece of the snake's head. Carefully spread the paint with a soft cloth instead of a brush. Using a cloth enables you to better control the paint, so that it doesn't run down the sides of the puzzle piece. Take care not to get any paint on the edges. Be sure to use a nontoxic paint becuase this is a child's project.

Step 13: Apply the alphabet. Using a ½" stencil or rub-on letters, apply the alphabet. Place the puzzle back into the scrap board as you work so the alphabet is placed on the snake's body in alphabetical order. Try to line up all letters the same way.

Step 14: Draw and paint the snake's eye. Using a pencil, lightly draw the eye in place. Then, using black paint, carefully paint the eye with a #00 round brush.

Step 15 (Optional): Apply a finish. Carefully apply a topcoat of clear gloss interior varnish or a similar product just on the top painted area of the snake.

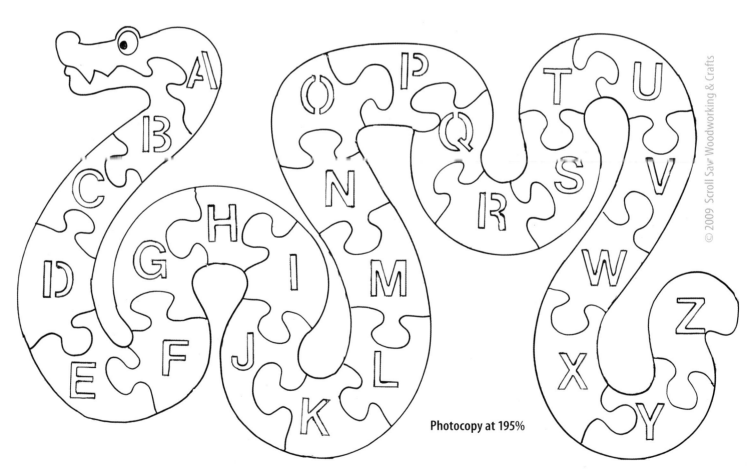

© 2009 Scroll Saw Woodworking & Crafts

Photocopy at 195%

Pocket-Size Tangram Puzzle

Clever puzzle-in-a-box provides a portable distraction

By Carl Hird-Rutter

Tangram puzzles, which the Chinese also call the Seven Boards of Cunning, can create an amazing number of designs using just seven tiles. This project includes two sets of tiles so you can play alone, creating more intricate designs, or play against an opponent, each using one set. The simple rules require you to use all seven tiles, and each tile must touch another tile.

The project is built in five ⅛"-thick layers, and it can easily be made in an evening. Cut the pieces to the rough size listed in the materials list. Sand all of the wood surfaces with progressively finer grits of sandpaper up to 220 grit. Permanently attach the front and back patterns to their respective blanks (see Attaching the Front and Back Patterns). Attach the puzzle drawer pattern to one of the blanks. Use masking tape or invisible tape to prepare a stack with the puzzle drawer pattern blank and two remaining blanks. Cut all three layers of the drawer section at the same time.

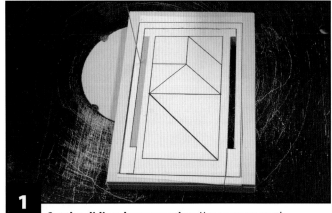

1 **Cut the sliding drawer section.** Use a reverse-tooth blade. Start on the outside edge, and cut around the perimeter of the drawer (the blue section). Remove the gray shaded pieces to allow the drawer to slide in and out of the stack. Separate the stack. Set the bottom blank aside.

2 **Cut the puzzle pieces.** Re-stack the top two pieces. Drill a blade entry hole in the innermost corner of the square tile. Cut along the lines to free all of the tiles. Make sure all of the corners remain sharp. Carefully place the pieces in order to make it easier to place them back inside the tray.

3 **Cut the top and bottom pieces.** Use a regular-tooth blade because the upturned teeth on a reverse-tooth blade will lift the pattern from the wood. Cut outside the line on everything but the finger access notches. The finishing cut will be done once the project is assembled.

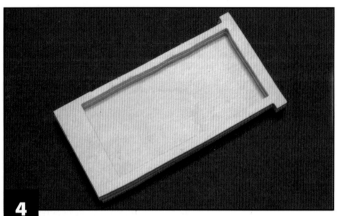

4 **Assemble the drawer.** Apply wood glue sparingly to the bottom of the two pieces that hold the tiles. Place these pieces on top of the drawer bottom. Once the pieces are aligned, clamp them in place and allow them to dry. Remove any excess glue that spills into the drawer.

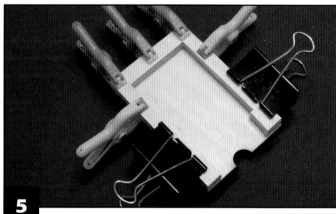

5 **Assemble the drawer sides.** Apply wood glue sparingly to the bottom of all three drawer side pieces (the yellow sections). Lay the bottom piece pattern side down and align the three layers on top. Clamp the four layers in place and allow them to dry. Remove any glue that squeezes out into the drawer area.

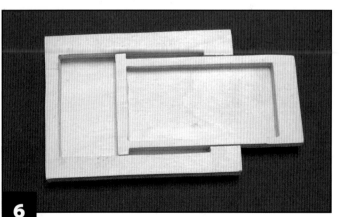

6 **Dry fit the drawer.** Sand the edges and bottom layer of the drawer. The drawer must be slightly thinner than the drawer sides. Fit the top layer in place and re-test the drawer, sanding again if needed. With the drawer in place, glue and clamp the top piece on the assembly. Note: the drawer protrudes from the case.

7 **Finish the puzzle.** Trim the sides of the box and the end of the drawer. Reduce the thickness of the tiles by running them along a sheet of 220-grit sandpaper on a sheet of glass. Do not round the corners. Put the tiles in position, and close the drawer.

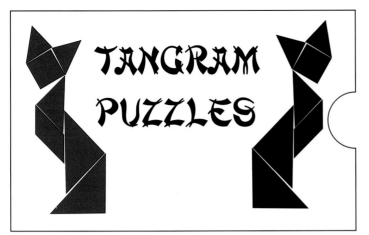

Top (1 piece)

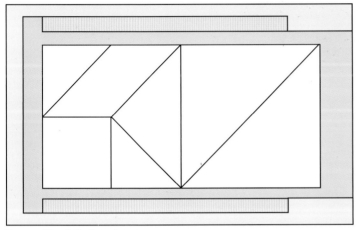

Drawer (Stack 3 pieces)

Bottom (1 piece)

Photocopy at 100%

© 2009 Scroll Saw Woodworking & Crafts

Attaching the Front and Back Patterns

The easiest way to attach the permanent patterns is to print them on a clear label, but over time, the adhesive may weaken. You can print the front and back designs on ordinary paper or vellum and apply a thin, even coat of spray adhesive to both the paper and the wood. Wait a few seconds until the adhesive is tacky and press the pattern onto the wood. Découpage is another technique. Apply a sealer, such as Mod Podge, to the back of the pattern, position it on the blank, and cover it with an additional coat of sealer.

I recommend using dark T-shirt transfers. Read the instructions because each brand is different. Place the transfer image-side-up onto the wood. Apply even pressure and heat it with a clothes iron for 45–60 seconds to release the transfer from the backing paper. A medium setting on the iron works best. Dark T-shirt transfer paper is available at office supply and craft stores.

PAINTING THE PROJECT   **TIP**

To keep the two sets of tiles separate, paint one set. Use acrylic paint and wipe off the excess so there is no buildup. If you apply too much paint, the drawer will not close properly. Sand any paint on the sides or bottoms of the tiles.

Materials & Tools

Materials:

- 5 pieces ⅛" x 3" x 4½" Baltic birch plywood
- Sandpaper, assorted grits up to 220 grit
- Spray adhesive (to attach drawer pattern)
- Large size clear label, dark T-shirt transfers, or découpage sealer, (to permanently attach the top and bottom patterns)
- Wood glue

- Acrylic craft paint
- Masking tape or invisible tape

Tools:

- #5 reverse-tooth and #5 regular-tooth blades or blades of choice
- Drill press with ⅟₁₆"-diameter bit
- Assorted small clamps

The images on the top and back of the puzzle box are from the typeface Textam-Piple, © Richard D. Parker & Apostrophic Laboratories. Derived from the Chinese game *ch'I ch' ae pan,* or "Seven-Board of Cunning." First printed in the time of Emperor Chia Ch'ing (1796-1820).

CREATE: The Word Game

A clever, easy-to-make puzzle

By Charles Bowman

When something sounds too good to be true, it usually is. This project, however, delivers everything it promises. It is easy to build, fun to play, and provides hours of entertainment. Given to a child, this clever word game serves as a learning tool. To a busy executive, it is seen as a gentle way to relieve stress.

I came up with the idea for the word game under somewhat stressful conditions. Despite the recurring nature of birthdays, I suddenly found myself with just one weekend to come up with a unique gift for my grandson. My first thought was to make a simple wooden puzzle for him. Then I realized I had already made him a puzzle for every birthday and every holiday. It was time for something different. But I was drawing the proverbial blank as I struggled to come up with the new "thing."

I decided to sleep on it, and sure enough, I woke up with a fresh idea. Since I wanted to create something special, I thought, why not integrate the word "create" into the project? I could cut out the six letters that spell the word and position them on something that would allow the letters to be easily rearranged. Once I had the concept, I went to my shop and began working. Soon I had the completed game, which I wrapped up and gave to my grandson. Would he like it? My question was answered when he tore through the paper, pulled out the pieces, and began playing with it right away. Follow these simple instructions, and you can create a special gift, too.

Step 1: Gather the wood. You will need six pieces for the letters, each measuring 2⅛" x 2½", so cut your stock now to form the basic starting blocks. I use hardwoods because they stand up to the abuse suffered from being handled, and they take a nice finish. I also prefer the ¾" thickness because it makes for a nice, solid letter to handle when forming different words. The wood I used for this particular project is macacauba.

Step 2: Attach the letter patterns. Put the patterns on the blocks, one letter per block. A removable glue stick works quite well. Once the pattern is attached to the wood, transfer the centerline from the pattern to the center of the bottom edge.

SAFETY FIRST **TIP**

This wooden word game is one you might want to make with a youngster. In addition to teaching him or her proper cutting techniques, you'll also want to promote safe work habits. Here are a couple of reminders to help keep you and your young ones safe in the shop: First, before beginning any project, clean your work area. Vacuuming and picking up scraps, as well as cleaning and sharpening your tools, all make for a safe working environment. Second, never try to concentrate when you are tired. Third, provide adult supervision whenever young woodworkers use anything that is plugged in, has teeth, or can cause injury. And, lastly, though it's not technically a safety tip, the rule of "measure twice, cut once" should be instilled in youngsters (and remembered by adults).

Step 3: Drill holes for the pegs. To hold the letters in place on the wooden base, use ¼" dowels as pegs. To make the peg hole, drill a ¼" hole centered on the bottom edge, ¼" deep. Repeat this process for all six letters.

Step 4: Drill a starting hole for the inside cuts. You'll need to do this on the two *e*'s and the *a* with a ⅛" bit. Make these cuts with a #9 skip-tooth blade. Use the same blade to make all of the outside cuts for each letter. Go slowly and stay on the lines. Once you have all six letters cut, get some 120-grit sandpaper and hand sand each one to round off all of the edges.

▲ **Step 5: Make the pegs.** Cut six pieces of ¼" dowel, each 1" long. Glue the pegs into the holes you drilled in each letter. Leave only ¾" of the peg exposed.

Step 6: Finish the letters. Apply your favorite finish to each letter. I use a clear gel varnish because I want the beauty of the wood grain to show. It's easy to apply. Just glob it on with a foam brush, let it sit for three to five minutes, and wipe off the excess with a lint-free paper towel. If you will be giving this game to a family with children small enough to chew on the pieces, paint them with a child-safe paint.

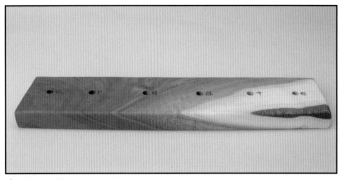

▲ **Step 7: Make the base.** Cut the wood of your choice to the dimensions on the pattern. (I like hardwoods, so I chose walnut for this particular piece.) The pattern also includes the measurements for drilling the ¼" peg holes. Drill the holes all the way through the base.

Step 8: Sand and finish the base. Sand and apply your favorite finish to the base. Once everything is dry, see how many words you can form using these six letters. You will be pleasantly surprised at the result. Enjoy.

Materials & Tools

Materials:
- 1 piece ¾" 16" x 2⅛" hardwood (letters)
- ¾" x 12" x 2½" hardwood (base)
- 6" x ¼" dowel (pegs)
- Removable glue stick
- Sandpaper, 120 and 220 grit
- Clear gel varnish (or finish of choice)
- Lint-free paper towel

Tools:
- #9 skip-tooth blade
- Drill with ⅛"-diameter bit
- Foam brush

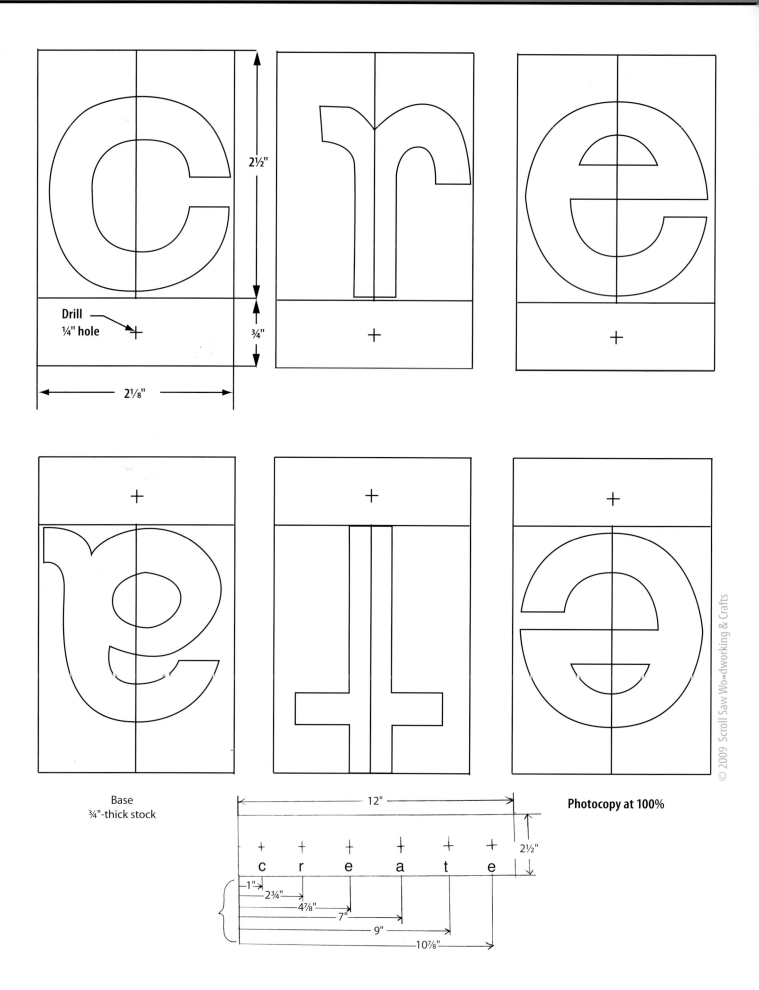

Drill ¼" hole

2½"

¾"

2⅛"

Base
¾"-thick stock

12"

2½"

c r e a t e

1"
2¾"
4⅞"
7"
9"
10⅞"

Photocopy at 100%

World's Most Difficult Four-Piece Puzzle

You'll make this quicker than people solve it

By Jim Stirling

The puzzle is more difficult to solve when all pieces are the same color. This puzzle is painted to make the assembly and solution photos easier to see.

This is a quick and inexpensive puzzle to make at shows, while attracting visitors to your booth. I've been making this puzzle for ten years and give similar versions to children and the young at heart. I made this one from a scrap piece of medium-density fiberboard (MDF).

After you scroll this puzzle, the trick is to get the four pieces apart and then put them together. It takes a child about four minutes to figure out how to take it apart and put it together while adults need about ten minutes to do so.

Step 1: Find the center and draw the patterns. Draw an *X* on the board from corner to corner. Then, draw lines across the center from the length and width to divide the wood into quarters. Draw four bell-shaped pieces. These pieces can be of various sizes as long as they interlock like a jigsaw puzzle.

Step 2: Cut the puzzle. Angle the scroll saw downward on the right. Take a small scrap piece of the same wood you plan to make the puzzle from. Saw this piece in two, using the bell-shaped cut. Slide the two pieces against each other until they lock. They must lock about halfway through. Keep adjusting the angle of the table and repeating the exercise until the two pieces are sliding about halfway through before locking. In our case, the angle was three degrees. This angle will

always vary depending upon the thickness of the material and the type of blade used. Once you have found the correct angle to cut the pieces, make the cuts with the actual wood you have set aside for the puzzle.

Step 3. Cut in from the four sides to the center so each piece has the form of a geometrical cone. You have found the correct angle to cut when ³/₄" pieces lock with about a ³/₁₆" overlap without sliding apart. Cut each line of the puzzle from the edge to the center, and then back out of the cut. Do not cut all the way across the puzzle following the line.

Taking Apart the Puzzle

▲ **Step 1: Lock the pieces.** The secret to taking the puzzle apart is to think of the four sections as two, two-part pieces. Slide one adjoining piece up and the other piece down until they lock. Do this with the other two pieces.

▲ **Step 2: Twist.** Gently twist two pieces downward and the other two pieces upward until you have two pieces of two, which you can then easily disassemble.

Putting the Puzzle Back Together

▲ **Step 1: Put the pairs together.** Put together the four pieces in pairs. Then, slide the pieces against each other until they lock.

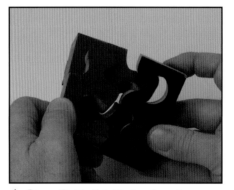

▲ **Step 2: Twist.** Twist the pieces so the smaller end of the taper is introduced into the large end of the taper and twist.

Photocopy at 100%

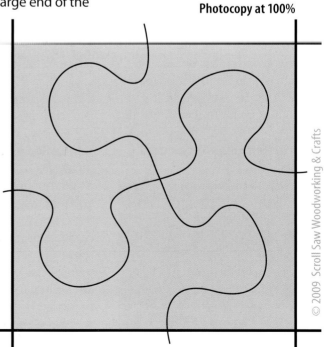

Apple Alphabet Puzzle

What child can resist a puzzle this brightly colored? She (or he) won't even know she's learning something!

Help youngsters learn their ABCs with this great alphabet puzzle.

By Joanne Lockwood

Show someone that they are the "apple" of your eye with this bright puzzle. Primary school teachers are always looking for stimulating, fun, and educational toys for their students, and they always appreciate a homemade gift. And since the pieces are so big, the puzzle will make a great gift for youngsters getting ready to start school!

Scroll this puzzle as a great end-of-the-year present for a favorite teacher.

Step 1: Cut the top and bottom puzzle to size. Stack them together with the ¾" piece on top and apply masking tape around the outside to secure.

Step 2: Apply the outside pattern. Only use gray graphite paper. Do not use carbon paper—it will run and smear when wet, and the lines cannot be erased. Gray graphite paper, made for painters, is erasable. Cut the two pieces out using the #5 blade. Separate and sand if needed.

Step 3: Seal all of the pieces. Apply sealer and let dry. Paint the entire top piece with two coats of tomato red—if you wait to paint it after you've cut out the letters, the paint will make the pieces hard to remove and put back in.

Step 4: Draw on the rest of the pattern. Add the alphabet, leaves, and stem using white graphite transfer paper (easier to see on the painted piece). Make sure you center the pattern exactly.

Step 5: Drill blade entry holes in each letter. Use the smallest drill bit that the #3 double-tooth blade will fit through.

Step 6: Cut out and remove the letters. Sand where necessary.

Step 7: Paint the bottom tomato red. Leave about 1" around the edges where it will be glued to the top section and allow it to dry.

Step 8: Glue the bottom to the top. Run a bead of glue around the entire outside and add a few drops between the letter holes. Align the two pieces and clamp securely. Use a damp cotton swab to remove any glue that oozed out. Allow it to dry.

Step 9: Drill holes in *A, B, D, O, P, Q,* and *R*. Use a ¼" drill bit and drill the holes ¼" deep as shown on the pattern.

Step 10: Paint the insides of the holes. Use a cotton swab dipped in tomato red.

Step 11: Paint all of the letters with lamp black. Do not paint the edges of the letters or let paint get down in the holes you just drilled. Paint the leaves with light green and shade around the edges with dark green. Dry brush a bit of the light green in the center to highlight if needed. Paint the veins with the dark green. Paint the stem with the light cinnamon.

Step 12: Finish the outside edges. Use an appropriate color and do any touch-up needed. To shade around the edge of the apple, add a touch of lamp black to the tomato red.

Step 13: Take the letters out and spray. Use a spray finish. Allow to dry overnight and insert the alphabet.

This design is not intended for children under 3 or who still put things in their mouths, as choking could result. Enlarge the pattern to a size suitable for the age and safety of your child.

Materials & Tools

Materials:
- ⅛" x 8" x 9" Baltic birch plywood (puzzle bottom)
- ¾" x 8" x 9" knot-free pine (puzzle top)

Tools:
- #3 double-tooth blades
- #5 double-tooth blades
- Drill with bits to fit blades
- Sandpaper, 150, 180, 220 grits
- Yellow wood glue
- 1" masking tape
- Small C-clamps
- Repositionable spray adhesive or graphite transfer paper in gray and white.
- Paintbrushes, such as Loew Correll Series 7150 La Cornell ¾" wash, Comfort Series 3000 #2 Round, Comfort Series 3000 #5 Round, Comfort Series 3400 ½" angular, Comfort Series 3400 ¾" Round.
- ¼"-diameter drill bit

Finishing Materials:
- Multi-purpose sealer
- Matte spray finish
- Acrylic paints in light green, dark green, light cinnamon, lamp black, and tomato red
- Brush tub
- Cotton swabs

Photocopy at 100%

Paul Bunyan
Tray Puzzle

Vivid colors bring this tall tale to life

By Russell Greenslade

Tall tales and legends have always fascinated me. Children are drawn to the colorful characters and entertaining stories. Spend some time with the special child in your life and have fun re-telling the story of Paul Bunyan as they work on assembling the puzzle.

I prefer to cut my puzzles from basswood because it has a plain grain and sands and finishes well. This piece is finished with thin washes of acrylic paint followed by an oil finish for durability.

Step 1: Prepare the blanks. Cut the blanks to the size listed in the materials list. Sand with progressively finer grits of sandpaper up to 220 grit. Adhere the pattern to one of the blanks.

Step 2: Drill a blade entry hole where indicated on the pattern. Drill a ⅛"-diameter hole for Babe's eye. Thread a #5 reverse-tooth blade

through the blade entry hole, and cut out the puzzle section. Do not cut through the frame.

Step 3: Cut the outside of the frame. Trace the frame perimeter onto the other blank, and cut along that line to make the backing board.

Step 4: Glue the frame onto the backing board. Use wood glue.

Step 5: Sand the pieces. Even up the backing board and frame. Use a belt sander to reduce the thickness of the sky by ⅜", the sun by ¼", the mountain by ³⁄₁₆", the trees and forest by ⅛", and all of Babe except for her ear by ¹⁄₁₆".

Step 6: Paint the puzzle pieces. Thin acrylic paint with water to the consistency of skim milk and paint the pieces. Use the picture as a guide or paint the pieces as desired.

Step 7: Apply an oil finish to the entire piece. Dip the pieces in your oil finish of choice; I use Danish oil, but pure tung oil is a good choice if the puzzle will be used by youngsters. Wipe the pieces with a soft rag, and set them aside to dry on paper towels.

Materials & Tools

Materials:
- 2 pieces ¾" x 8½" x 10½" basswood or wood of choice
- Assorted grits of sandpaper up to 220 grit
- Acrylic paint of choice
- Oil finish of choice
- Paper towels

Tools:
- #5 reverse-tooth blades or blades of choice
- Drill with ⅛"- and ¹⁄₁₆"-diameter drill bits
- Belt sander or sander of choice
- Paintbrushes of choice

Blade entry hole

Photocopy at 100%

Dairy Delight Puzzle

Travel-size puzzle provides hours of toddler fun

By Joanne Lockwood

To put it in county fair terms, this project's a blue ribbon winner. You'll have a great time cutting the cow puzzle, and children will have fun putting it together and taking it apart. It's also a great visual aid showing youngsters the many different types of food that come from cows. This is a great gift, but it is not meant for tots who still put objects in their mouths. To avoid such a circumstance, enlarge the pattern accordingly.

Step 1: Prepare the wood. Cut all three pieces of wood to size. Sandwich them in the order given in the materials list—top, center, and bottom. Use masking tape to secure around the edges. Adhere the cow pattern to the top piece with spray glue. Spray only the pattern, not the wood.

Step 2: Cut and sand. Cut out the project. Remove the tape. Sand and seal all three pieces with multi-purpose sealer. It is best to do the sealing before the puzzle pieces are cut. You do not want to seal inside the holes, as the pieces will not come out if the grain is raised. Let dry. Re-sand.

Step 3: Trace all of the patterns. Then, adhere the pattern for the puzzle pieces to the ½"-thick piece of wood with spray glue or transfer paper. Do not use carbon paper!

Step 4: Drill entry holes and cut puzzle pieces. Using your smallest drill bit, drill blade entry holes next to each puzzle piece. Insert one end of a #5 double-tooth blade into the hole you drilled by the cheese, re-tension your blade, and cut the piece out. Repeat this process until all the puzzle pieces are cut out. Leave the pieces out. Put a thin line of glue on the underside of this piece, align it with the ⅛"-thick bottom piece and clamp. Using a wet cotton swab, remove any excess glue. Do not put the pieces back in. Let dry.

Step 5: Sand all of the small pieces well. Especially sand the edges if necessary. If you used a new blade when cutting, sanding will probably not be necessary at this point.

Step 6: Align all three pieces. Use the ¼"-diameter bit to drill a hole in the ear for the axle peg, which is indicated by the X on the pattern. Insert the peg through the top piece, add a tiny drop of glue to the tip of the peg, and insert it into the hole.

Painting Notes

I have painted two versions of this piece. One has very basic painting, for which directions are included. More advanced painters may want to shade where shown on the other version. I do not recommend painting the edges of the pieces. I did and had to really sand to get them to slip out easily.

Using the largest brush, basecoat all of the three main pieces in white wash except the top of the ½"-thick (center) piece. Wash the top of that piece with soft black by diluting the paint with water to an inky consistency, which allows the grain to show through. Try not to get any in the holes. Allow this paint to dry.

Next, paint the front of the cow and the puzzle pieces. Let this paint dry before applying the detail ink with the Micron pen. At this point, allow the paint to dry overnight. Then, apply just a misting of matte spray finish with the puzzle pieces out of the cow. I used a matte finish on mine, but you can use a high-gloss finish if you prefer. All products I used are nontoxic when dry.

PAINTING PALETTE USING ACRYLICS AND SATINS

Cow Front: Apply pattern with graphite paper.
Spots/tip of tail: Soft black
Hooves/horns/eyelids: Toffee
Snout/udder/inside ears: Hi-lite flesh
Nostrils: Dusty rose
All liner work can be done with soft black and a liner brush or the .005 Micron pen. Be sure to skip areas. It looks better than a solid line.

Puzzle Pieces:

American cheese: Cadmium yellow
Swiss cheese: White wash to lighten
Butter: Cadmium yellow
Milk can/heart: Shimmering silver/ country red
Cottage cheese/lid: Country red/ white wash
Cone: Terra cotta
Ice cream: Country red/mink tan
Cream and milk cartons: White wash, milk carton also has mink tan center
Steak: White wash country red with touch of soft black; brush mix it on your palette
Yogurt: Mink tan

All details are done with the Micron pen.

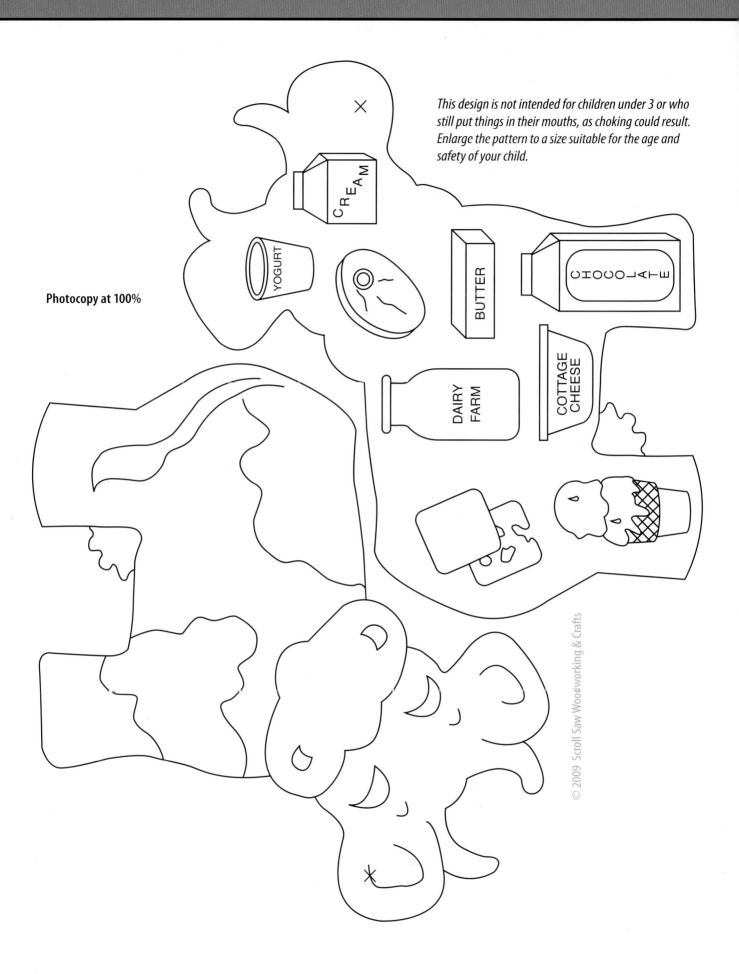

This design is not intended for children under 3 or who still put things in their mouths, as choking could result. Enlarge the pattern to a size suitable for the age and safety of your child.

Photocopy at 100%

© 2009 Scroll Saw Woodworking & Crafts

Apply black paint and cutting lines disappear

By Tom Zieg

The Ultimate Puzzle

The making of this puzzle is quite simple, really. But putting it together will drive your friends mad. The next time you want to create a stir, give this puzzle as a present or get it out at a party. How good are your puzzle-solving skills? Check the handy chart to find out.

Step 1: Prepare the wood. Using a rag, dampen the top surface of the board with water to raise the grain. When dry, sand with 220-grit sandpaper and, once smooth, wipe down with a tack rag. Spray paint with black latex paint. After the first coat has dried, sand with 220-grit sandpaper and wipe off any dust. Then, apply a second coat. Finish the preparation by applying a clear spray finish.

Step 2: Affix the pattern to the black surface. Use temporary bond spray adhesive.

Step 3: Cut the puzzle. Make sure you make the first five cuts in the order shown on the pattern. The suggested cutting order will segment the puzzle into five sections and eliminate the need for any 90° turns. The first cut divides the puzzle into two pieces, making it easier to cut on a 16" saw. Be sure you cut completely through the puzzle sections. Also, make sure you don't make any 90° turns. Sharp turns like that will leave little gaps from the blade that interrupt the smooth flow of the puzzle lines. Those gaps can give the person assembling the puzzle hints of where the pieces go.

So how good are you?

Completion Time	Rating
More than a month	"C'mon man, what's the hold up?"
2 weeks to a month	"Oh, well. At least it wasn't longer."
1 to 2 weeks	"Movin' right along, aren't we?"
1 day to 1 week	"Hey, you're pretty good."
Less than 1 day	"Did you cheat?"

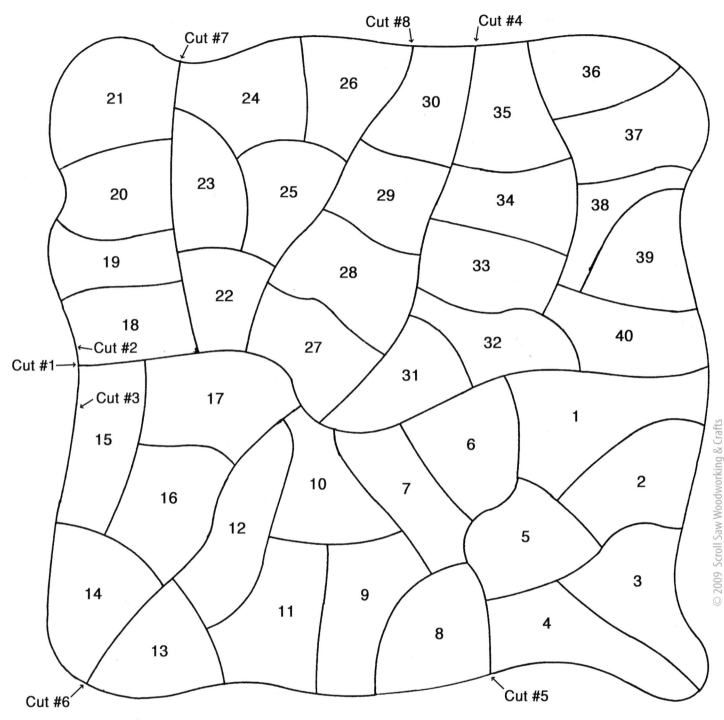

Cut #7 Cut #8 Cut #4

21 24 26 30 35 36

23 25 29 34 37

20 38

19 28 33 39

22

18 27 32 40

Cut #2
Cut #1

Cut #3 17 31

15 6 1

16 10 7

5 2

12

14 9 3

11 4

13 8

Cut #6 Cut #5

© 2009 Scroll Saw Woodworking & Crafts

Photocopy at 100%

MAKING THE PUZZLE MORE DIFFICULT TO ASSEMBLE

TIP

Paint both sides of the puzzle and it really becomes difficult to assemble. Prepare the bottom surface as detailed in Step 1. Use temporary bond spray adhesive to affix a piece of paper to the completely dried bottom surface to protect it from damage as you cut it on the saw.

Climbing Cats

A beautiful and whimsical standing puzzle

By John A. Nelson

I noticed some clever puzzles in a local store and was inspired to create my own design. Cats are always popular projects and seemed a fitting subject for this whimsical puzzle. Once all the pieces are put together, the puzzle will stand on its own.

The pieces are big enough that children can play with it safely, but the design—and challenge to assemble it—make it fun for adults as well. If you cut it out of hardwood, finishing can be as easy as a coat of tung oil or Danish oil.

Materials & Tools

Materials:
- ½" x 8" x 9" hardwood
- Sandpaper, assorted grits
- Temporary bond spray adhesive
- Tung oil, Danish oil, or finish of choice

Tools
- #5 reverse-tooth blade
- Drill with ¹⁄₁₆"-diameter bit
- Brush or rag

Photocopy at 160%

T-Rex Dinosaur Puzzle

This popular design is simple to make

By William Berry

This whimsical dinosaur puzzle is sure to be a hit with any child—and many adults as well! The finished puzzle looks equally nice painted or cut from hardwoods and left natural. The simple lines make it easy for scrollers of any skill level to create custom-crafted gifts for the holiday season.

I began scroll sawing puzzles for Christmas gifts after picking up the book *Make Your Own Model Dinosaurs* by Danny A. Downs. At 3 a.m. on Christmas morning, I was still putting on the finishing touches. I enjoyed crafting the puzzles but was looking for something less complex.

I soon discovered the work of Judy and Dave Peterson in *Scroll Saw Woodworking & Crafts*. Their puzzles were quite unique and took a lot less time to produce. When a co-worker asked me for a dinosaur puzzle as a gift for her niece, I was excited to design a puzzle in the Petersons' style. She suggested a "goofy" type of dinosaur, because it was for a younger child.

Before cutting a puzzle, make sure your scroll saw table is square to the blade. Otherwise, the puzzle pieces will not pass freely through each other. Decide whether you will paint your dinosaur or cut the puzzle from hardwood and use an oil finish or stain.

Transfer the pattern to the blank. Drill blade entry holes for the eye and nostrils. These parts are cut first. Cut the line that forms the teeth and smile before cutting the head free. Cut through to the bottom end of the smile line. Then, back the blade out and turn it to make the upper line. Rather than trying to back the blade all the way out, turn off the saw and remove the blade from the piece. Cut the pieces, then sand each piece and round them over with a flap sander.

You can finish the dinosaur with a simple solid color or get creative by adding shading and details.

Painting the Dinosaur

Decide how much detail you want to add. For a simple paint job, apply the base color to the entire puzzle. I roll the paint over the edges to the point where the rounding ends; that way no wood shows between the pieces when the puzzle is assembled. Then, paint the eye, belly, and markings. For a more artistic look, add highlights and shadows with different shades of the base coat. Tint the base color with just a spot of black paint. Apply it in areas to create shadows around the dinosaur's features. Then, add a touch of white to the base color to create highlights. You may need to wash the original base coat color over the shadows and highlights to tone them down.

After the paint has been allowed to dry, apply a clear coat to protect the puzzle.

Photocopy at 100%

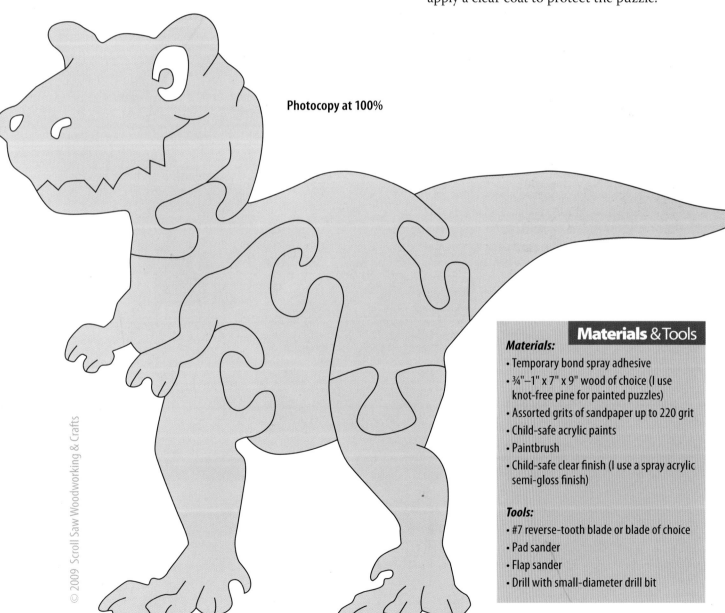

Materials & Tools

Materials:
- Temporary bond spray adhesive
- ¾"–1" x 7" x 9" wood of choice (I use knot-free pine for painted puzzles)
- Assorted grits of sandpaper up to 220 grit
- Child-safe acrylic paints
- Paintbrush
- Child-safe clear finish (I use a spray acrylic semi-gloss finish)

Tools:
- #7 reverse-tooth blade or blade of choice
- Pad sander
- Flap sander
- Drill with small-diameter drill bit

Ingenious Animal Family Puzzles

Kids will go wild for these charming and easy-to-make nested puzzles

Cut by Ben Fink

With the increasing concerns about toxic paint on children's toys, these stylish, Asian-inspired animal puzzles make a popular and safe gift choice. The simple nesting designs are easy to cut, attractive, and fun to put together. If the puzzles are intended for children under three years of age, make sure to enlarge the patterns to avoid any choking hazards.

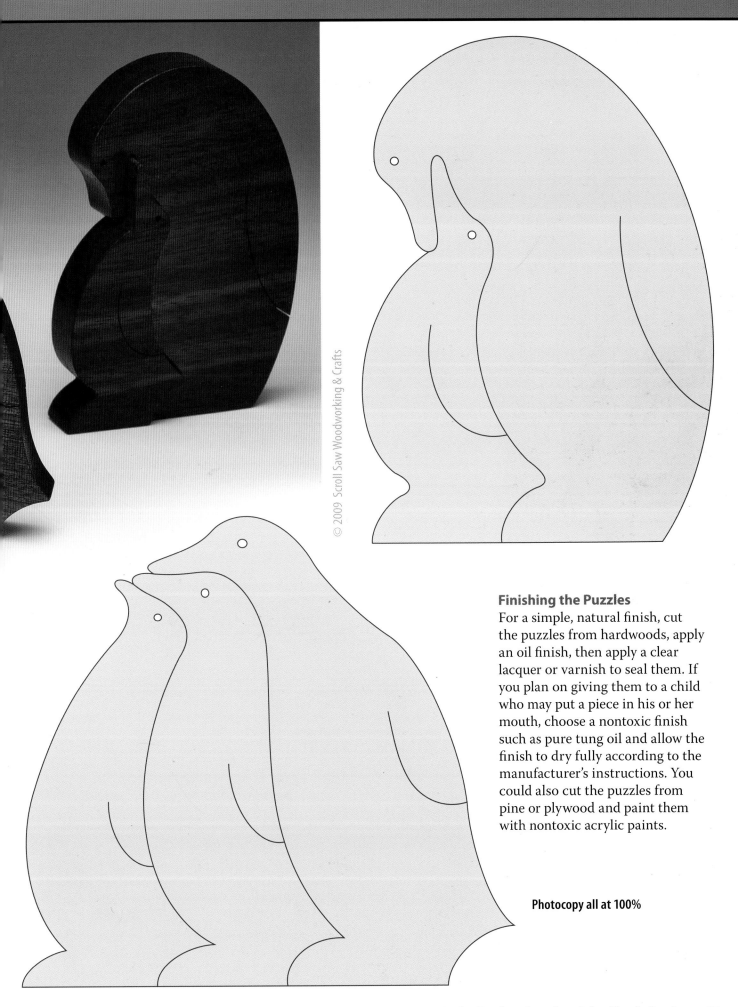

Finishing the Puzzles

For a simple, natural finish, cut the puzzles from hardwoods, apply an oil finish, then apply a clear lacquer or varnish to seal them. If you plan on giving them to a child who may put a piece in his or her mouth, choose a nontoxic finish such as pure tung oil and allow the finish to dry fully according to the manufacturer's instructions. You could also cut the puzzles from pine or plywood and paint them with nontoxic acrylic paints.

Photocopy all at 100%

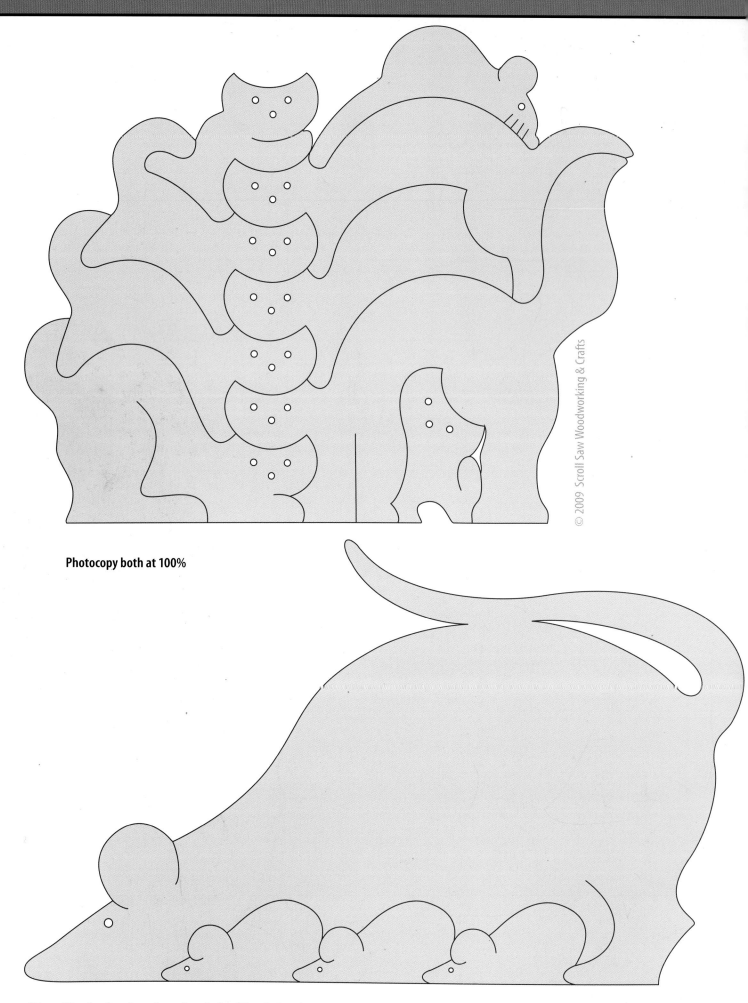

Photocopy both at 100%

Stack cut the puzzles from contrasting hardwoods to add dimension to the project.

Materials & Tools

Materials:

- ¾" x 4¾" x 7¾" hardwood or wood of choice (mice)
- ¾" x 5½" x 7½" hardwood or wood of choice (cats)
- ¾" x 4½" x 7½" hardwood or wood of choice (elephants)
- ¾" x 4½" x 8" hardwood or wood of choice (zebras)
- ¾" x 4" x 6½" hardwood or wood of choice (penguin group)
- ¾" x 5" x 5½" hardwood or wood of choice (penguin trio)
- ¾" x 4" x 5½" hardwood or wood of choice (penguin pair)
- Assorted grits of sandpaper
- Finish of choice

Tools:

- #5 skip-tooth blades or blades of choice
- Drill with ⅛"-diameter and ¹⁄₁₆"-diameter drill bits (eye holes and blade entry holes)
- Brushes to apply finish (optional)

Highlight natural puzzles by using figured wood to simulate textures.

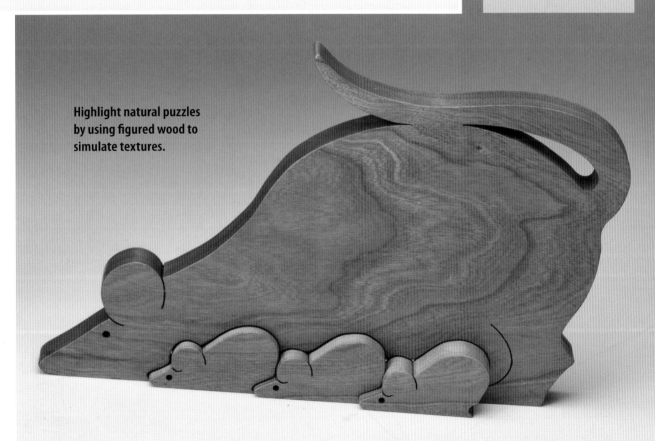

Photocopy both at 100%

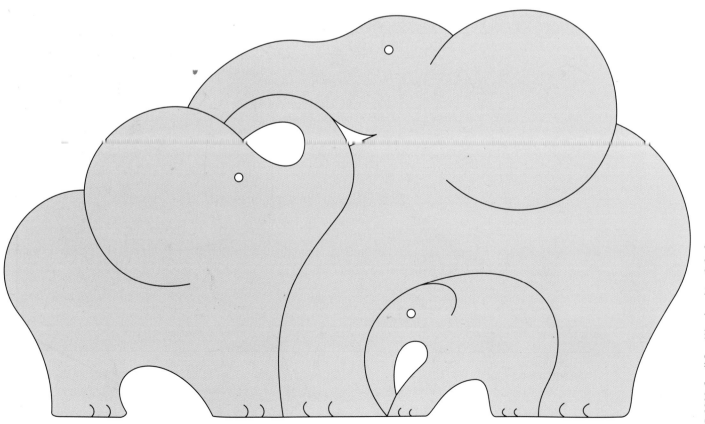

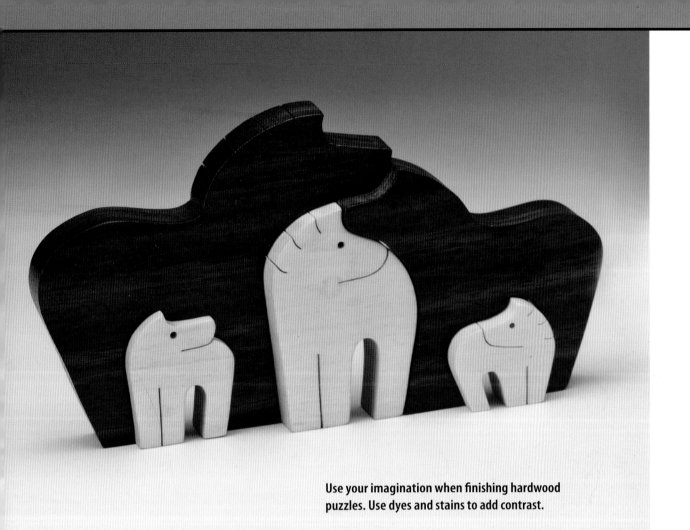

Use your imagination when finishing hardwood puzzles. Use dyes and stains to add contrast.

Apply a food-safe oil finish to bring out the beauty in the wood.

Intermediate Puzzles

The puzzles shown in this section are a little more advanced than the beginner puzzles, but they're worth the extra effort once you have developed your skills. All of the projects featured have all of the information you need to complete them. For some, that includes full step-by-step instructions; for others, all you'll need is simply the pattern, photo, and materials list.

Woodimal Lion by James W. Sweet, page 60.

Wizard Puzzle

These colorful and unique designs will delight collectors and makers

By Russell Greenslade

When I design puzzles, I look for inspiration everywhere—whether it's the oceans around me or stories in books. These two puzzles are interpretations of some common fantasy elements.

For my puzzles, I use basswood because it has a uniform grain, it sands well, and it cuts easily. Basswood also works well with the wood dyes, thin acrylic washes, and Danish oil I use to give my puzzles their distinct look. When you cut any puzzles, I recommend using reverse-tooth blades because they will help reduce your sanding time.

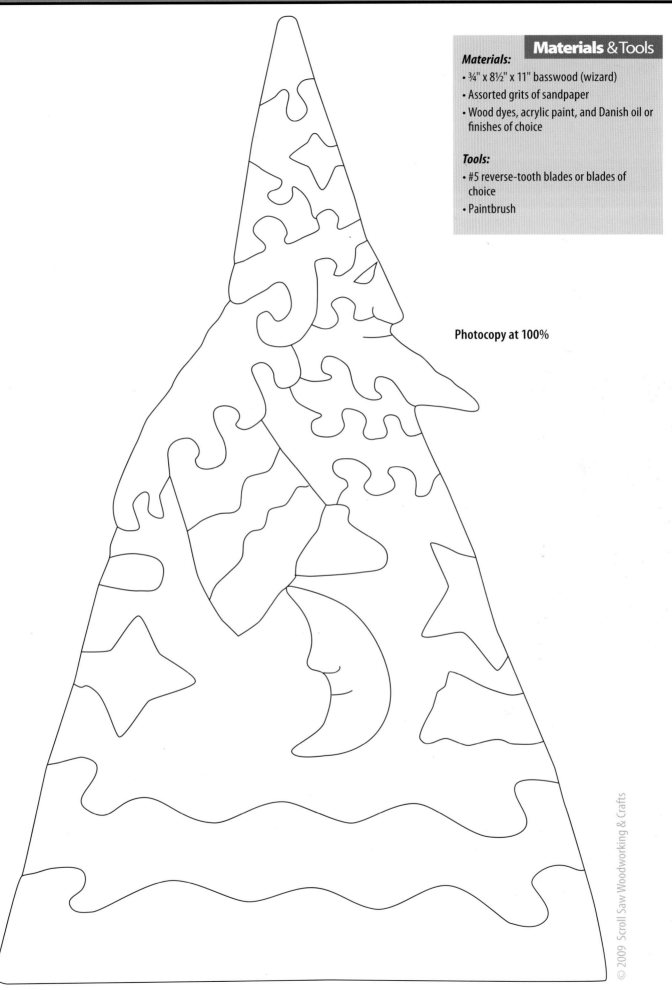

Photocopy at 100%

Star Puzzle

Materials & Tools

Materials:
- ¾" x 8" x 8" basswood (star)
- Assorted grits of sandpaper
- Wood dyes, acrylic paint, and Danish oil or finishes of choice

Tools:
- #5 reverse-tooth blades or blades of choice
- Paintbrush

Photocopy at 125%

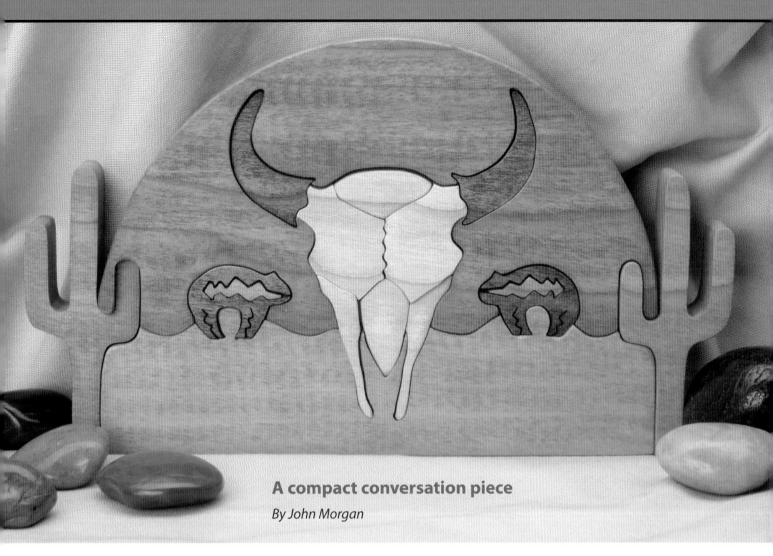

A compact conversation piece

By John Morgan

Southwestern Puzzle

Regardless of where you live, you're sure to know someone who has a house or apartment that features a southwestern motif in at least one room. At less than a foot wide and just under six inches tall, this compact puzzle makes a great conversation piece, perfectly sized for any size room or office. Please note that as presented here, the puzzle is not intended to be a child's toy. If you'd like to give it to a child, make sure you use child-safe paints and stains and enlarge the pieces so they cannot be swallowed.

Step 1: Attach the pattern. Use temporary bond spray adhesive to adhere the pattern to the wood. If possible, mount the bottom of the pattern at the edge of the board.

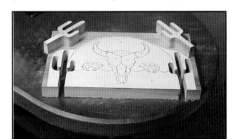

▲ **Step 2: Begin cutting.** Start by cutting the two cactus pieces from the blank. Use a #5 blade. A #2 blade can be used if you aren't comfortable making the tight turns with the #5.

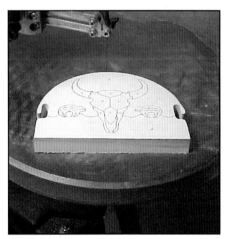

▲ **Step 3: Cut the waste.** Cut off the waste found over the top of the sun.

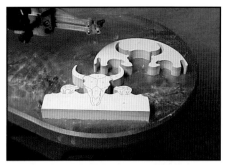

▲ Step 4: Cut the background. Cut out the sun by entering at the "horizon" on either side and following the dashed line on the pattern.

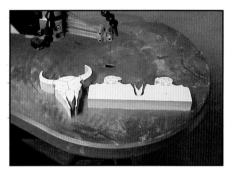

▲ Step 5: Cut out the skull. Cut the skull from the blank.

Step 6: Cut out the skull segments. Cut the segments of the skull according to the pattern lines.

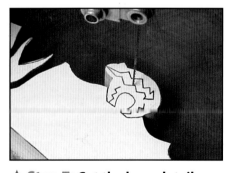

▲ Step 7: Cut the bear details. The bears can be left solid, without the arrows and zigzags. If you choose to cut out the arrows, do so while the bears are still attached to the large bottom puzzle piece. Note that once you cut the arrows, the bears will be very fragile.

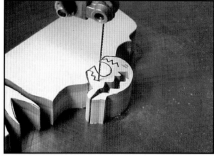

▲ Step 8: Cut out the bears. Cut the bears from the bottom piece, cutting into and backing out of the zigzag kerfs in the legs as you come to them.

Step 9: Remove the pattern. Peel away the paper pattern from each piece.

▲ Step 10: Sand the puzzle pieces. Use 150-grit sandpaper. I like to sand each individual piece by holding the sander upside down and bringing the pieces to the sander (watch your fingertips). You may, however, choose to sand the entire puzzle at one time. Simply assemble the puzzle, lay it flat on a nonskid surface, and sand all of the pieces at once (the arrows in the bears have a tendency to jump out). Make sure you sand both sides of the puzzle.

▲ Step 11: Remove sharp edges. Use a folded or rolled piece of sandpaper held at a slight angle to knock off the sharp edges of each piece. This helps define the lines when the puzzle is assembled and also removes any "fuzz" that may be left on the back edges of the pieces.

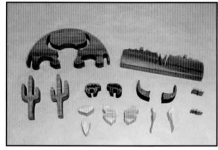

▲ Step 12: Stain and finish. Using the color key, stain each piece of the puzzle according to the stain manufacturer's instructions. After the stain is completely dry, apply a clear coating of your choice, if you desire.

ATTRACTIVE GRAINS MAKE GREAT PUZZLES	TIP

Any light-colored wood works great for this puzzle. I, however, usually choose poplar, especially if I find a piece with interesting mineral streaks. It really adds to the "character" of the puzzle. Other woods with interesting grains include cypress, as well as some pines and maples. Stay away from dark woods like oak, walnut, and mahogany, as the stains won't show up well.

FINISHING OPTIONS

Rather than the pigmented oil stains, you could use good watercolors or water-based aniline dyes. If you choose one of these options, you will have to sand the raised grain after the first staining has dried. Then, give each piece a second staining.

Wood grain

Photocopy at 100%

© 2009 Scroll Saw Woodworking & Crafts

Teacher's Puzzle

Personalized puzzle makes a unique commemorative gift

By Judy and Dave Peterson

This fun puzzle makes a great gift for your favorite student or teacher. Each piece can be personalized with a student's name as long as the class isn't too large. There is a limit to the number of pieces you can get from one board, but you could always make a pair of apples, if necessary.

We received an e-mail from a previous customer, Connie Karman. Her daughter was about to graduate from pre-school, and her daughter's class had 17 children in it. She asked if we could design and make an apple-shaped puzzle with pieces that the children could print their names on.

We suggested adding a stem for the teacher's name and a Staedtler Medium Tip indelible pen to print their names on the puzzle.

Disassemble the puzzle and let each child select a piece without anyone knowing in advance which piece goes where. The kids had fun printing their names on the pieces, and the gift was happily received by the teacher.

I use padauk for the puzzle and cover the stock with clear packaging tape before cutting to help lubricate the blade. Round the edges of each piece for a pleasing presentation and to avoid any sharp edges for little hands to cut themselves on. I use a flap sander, but you could also hand sand the edges. Apply a clear finish to protect the project. I recommend clear, outdoor Danish oil with a UV blocker.

Adding or reducing the number of pieces

With a little bit of work, you can adapt this pattern for smaller or larger classes.

Copy the pattern, enlarging or reducing the outline to fit your board of choice. Use a pencil with soft lead to divide the apple into rows. Then sketch in the appropriate number of columns. Keep an eraser handy. After you're done with that, go back and draw in the keys. Remember that the head of the key needs to be larger than the neck. Also, you need to have a key wherever one piece lies above, below, or next to another.

Design, cut, sand, finish, and enjoy the accolades from a grateful teacher, who will have been spared one more handkerchief or bottle of cheap perfume.

Materials & Tools

Materials:
- ¾" x 8" x 9½" wood of choice (I use padauk for its red color)
- Clear packaging tape
- Clear, outdoor Danish oil with a UV blocker
- Assorted grits of sandpaper up to 220 grit

Tools:
- #7 reverse-tooth blades or blades of choice
- Flap sander (optional)
- Staedtler Medium Tip indelible pen

Photocopy at 100%

Noah's Ark Puzzle

We asked decorative painter Donna Lloyd to add her special touch to the ark. If you aren't comfortable with duplicating her painting techniques, you can use simple primary colors to give the project its own personality.

Colored patterns make finishing this puzzle child's play

By Carl Hird-Rutter
Ark painted by Donna Lloyd

Noah's Ark is one of the best-known and most-loved Bible stories. Toys based on this beloved story have been childhood favorites for centuries. This version combines the classic toy with a simple puzzle suitable for children of any age.

The entire project is made of ½"-thick Baltic birch plywood. You can leave the animals as simple silhouettes or paint them with bright primary colors. The real beauty of this project is that you can use the colored animal patterns as the final finish. There are several methods to attach the patterns to the blanks (see sidebar).

Start by cutting your stock to size. Sand all of the surfaces and the edges with 180-grit sandpaper. Remove the dust with a tack cloth. I recommend plywood for added strength and durability.

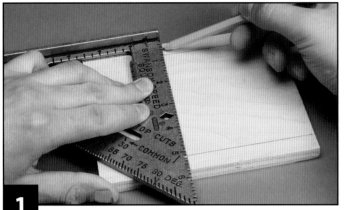

1

Attach the animal patterns. Create a T-shape for the animal blanks by removing a ⁹⁄₁₆" wide x 3¾" long tab from both sides. Attach the animal patterns (see sidebar). Any pattern extending beyond the cut animal can be sanded off after the piece is cut. Drill blade-entry holes for each of the animals. Square your saw table to the blade.

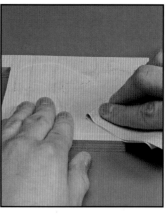

2

Cut the tabs and animals. Cut along the pattern with a #5 reverse-tooth blade. Once a blank is complete, test fit the animals. They should pass freely through the block from both directions. If a piece binds a little, trim the inside of the blank slightly for a better fit. With the animals in the blank, sand the back with 220-grit sandpaper and remove the dust with a tack cloth.

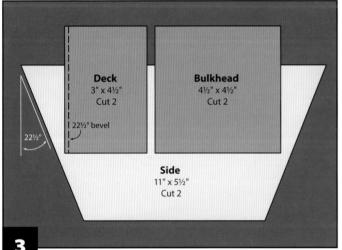

3

Cut out the ark. Cut the ark pieces according to the diagram above. The decks are cut with a 22½°-bevel on the outside. Use a miter saw or cut the bevel on the scroll saw by setting the saw table to a 22½°-angle. Trim one deck to 3". Dry assemble the ark and all of the animals to determine the width of the other deck.

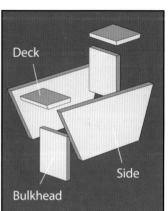

4

Assemble the ark. Use wood glue and finishing nails. Paint the ark as desired, then finish the ark, the blanks and the animals with a durable spray varnish. Allow the finish to cure for at least 30 days. For young children, omit the smaller animals, such as the penguins, that present a choking hazard. You could also add axles, wheels, and a string to turn the ark into a pull toy.

Attaching the color patterns

The easiest way to attach the animal patterns is to print them on an 8½" x 11" label, but over time, the adhesive may weaken. You can also print the animals on ordinary paper and apply a thin, even coat of spray adhesive to both the paper and the wood. Wait a few seconds until the adhesive is tacky, and press the pattern onto the wood. Découpage is another technique. Apply a sealer such as Mod Podge to the back of the pattern, position it on the blank, and cover it with an additional coat of Mod Podge.

I recommend using dark T-shirt transfers. Read the instructions as each brand of transfer paper is different. Place the transfer image-side-up onto the wood. Apply even pressure and heat it with a clothes iron for 45-60 seconds to release the transfer from the backing paper. A medium setting on the iron works best.

Materials & Tools

Materials:
- 8 each ½" x 5½" x 4½" Baltic birch plywood (animals)
- 4 each ½" x 5½" x 6¼" Baltic birch plywood (animals)
- 2 each ½" x 5½" x 11" Baltic birch plywood (sides)
- 2 each ½" x 3¼" x 4½" Baltic birch plywood (decks)
- 2 each ½" x 4½" x 4½" Baltic birch plywood (bulkheads)
- Sandpaper, 180 and 220 grit
- Tack cloth
- Dark T-shirt transfer paper, self-adhesive paper, or good quality paper (colored animals)

- Mod Podge (optional)
- Spray adhesive (optional)
- Non-toxic paint and spray varnish suitable for a child's toy

Tools:
- #5 or #7 reverse-tooth blades or blades of choice
- Miter saw (optional)
- Drill press with ¹⁄₁₆"-diameter drill bit

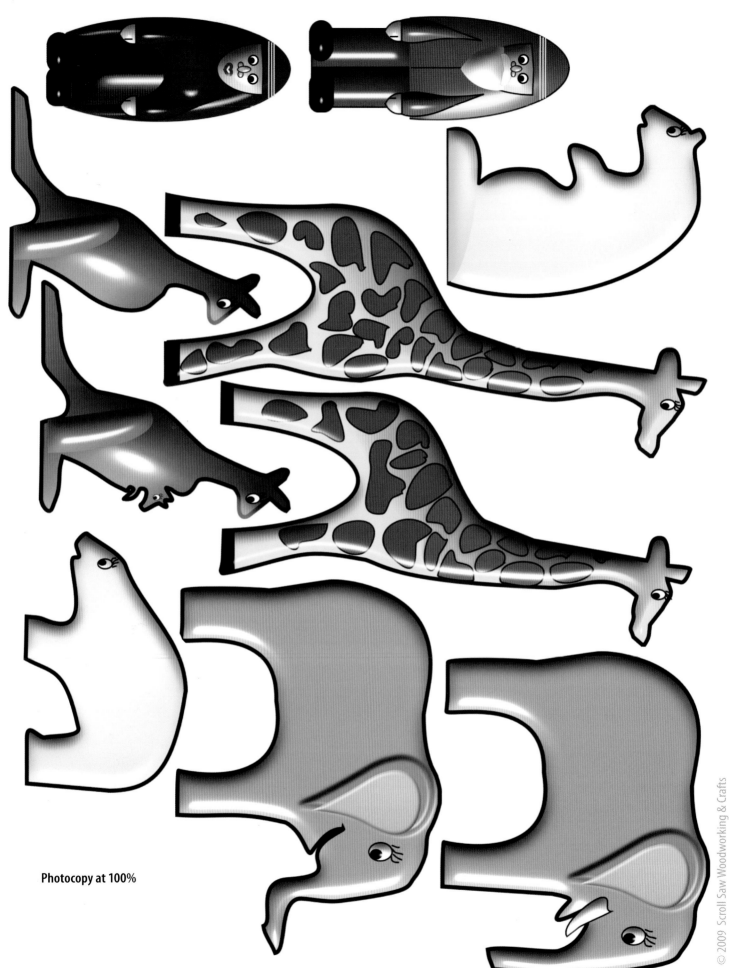

Photocopy at 100%

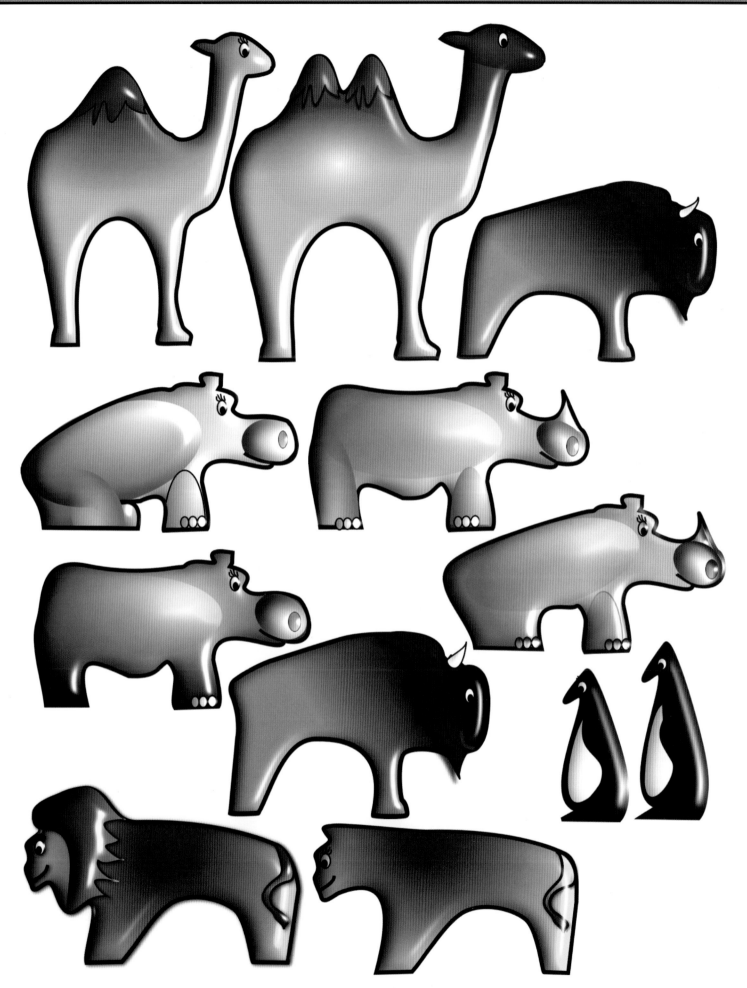

F-14 Swingwing *Puzzle*

When not in flight, the F-14 makes a challenging puzzle for kids of all ages.

With dowels inserted as pivot points, the wings can be moved to the open or closed position.

Impressive 3-D aircraft puzzle is easy to make

By Jim Sonnleitner

This model of a Navy F-14 Tomcat, complete with moving wings, is sure to be at the top of many Christmas wish lists. The Tomcat has been flying from aircraft carriers since the 1970s and has been continuously updated to be a modern fighting machine.

This creative puzzle combines two of my greatest loves—airplanes and scrolling. I enjoy making puzzles that are fun to play with—something other than a flat puzzle.

Start by stacking three pieces of ¼"-thick plywood together, using your method of choice. I use ⅝"-long brads. Apply temporary bond spray adhesive to the patterns, and attach them to the stack. All three patterns should fit on the plywood.

Next, drill ¼"-diameter holes through the stack where indicated on the pattern. I use a brad-point bit to reduce the chances of the bit wandering.

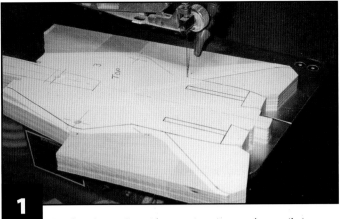

1 **Cut the pieces.** Set aside two wing pieces and two tail pieces; the third of each will not be used. Cut only the outline of the fuselage, or body. Separate the layers and mark them top, middle, and bottom.

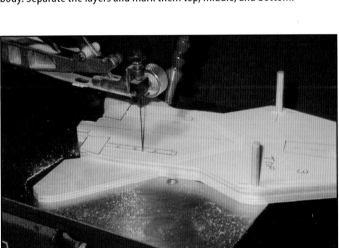

2 **Prepare the dowel pins.** Cut four ¼"-diameter dowels to 2" lengths. Put a slight chamfer on both ends of the dowels. I use a school pencil sharpener, but you can also sand the chamfer onto the dowels. These will serve as pins to keep the layers aligned as the project progresses.

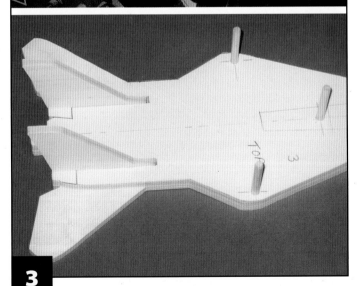

3 **Shape the main fuselage.** Stack the top and bottom layers together and secure these layers with the dowels. The middle layer should not be in this stack. Cut off the horizontal tail sections. Discard these sections. Disassemble the layers and restack the top and middle layers together. Secure these with the dowels. The bottom layer should not be in this stack. Drill ⅛"-diameter blade entry holes and cut the slots for the vertical tail fins. Test the fit of the tail fins in the slots, and adjust the slots as needed.

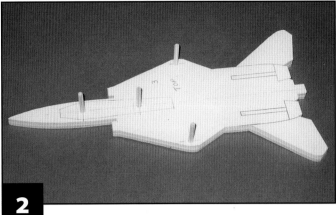

4 **Cut the canopy.** Stack all three layers of the fuselage and peg them together from the bottom with the dowels. Attach the canopy pattern to the canopy blank. Tape the canopy blank in position on top of the top layer. Set up the drill press to stop ¼" from the drill press platform. Flip the assembled stack over, and drill ¼"-diameter holes through the two existing holes in the nose of the airplane into the canopy. Remove one dowel at a time to drill into the canopy so you maintain your alignment. Do not drill completely through the canopy. Remove the canopy, keeping the three fuselage layers in order. Then, re-drill the four holes through the stack with a ⁹⁄₃₂"-diameter drill bit. Keep the layers aligned properly by removing the dowel only as you drill that hole.

5 **Cut the middle layer.** Transfer the pattern to the blank. Cut out the sections and mark the top of each piece. The middle section of the middle layer will be discarded to allow room for the wings to pivot.

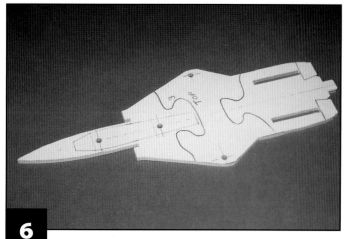

6 **Cut the top layer.** Darken the light lines that show the puzzle lobes. Cut along these lines to separate the top into three sections.

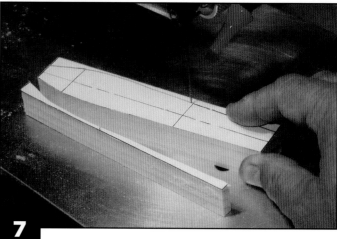

7 **Cut the canopy.** Cut the top view of the canopy. Tape the side pieces back into place. Then, cut the angled front and back pieces. Remove the paper pattern. Round over all the edges of the canopy with a sander. I use a belt sander, but you can also sand it by hand.

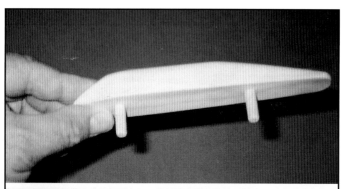

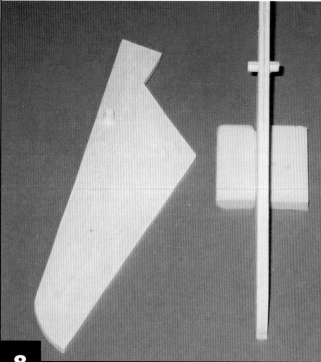

8 **Position the dowels.** Cut two of the ¼" dowels to 1¼" long. Insert them into the canopy holes. The ends should not extend more than ¾". Bevel the ends as needed. Glue them into place. Cut two ¼" dowels to ¾" length. Glue them in the wings so that ¼" extends out on either side. Be sure to wipe off any excessive glue. Put the puzzle together, and check the swinging action of the wings. Adjust the wings if needed.

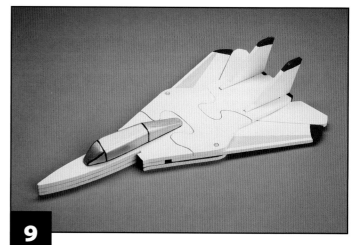

9 **Paint the puzzle.** The paint scheme I use is similar to the military Air Superiority Blue. A light blue blends with the sky. I paint each layer a different color as a hint for putting the puzzle together. Paint the top a light blue, the middle a medium blue, and the bottom a darker blue. I add a little trim color to brighten the aircraft and paint the canopy silver. Apply a clear sealer over all the surfaces.

Materials &Tools

Materials:
- 3 pieces ¼" x 8¾" x 16½" birch plywood (body, wings, and fins)
- ¾" x 1¼" x 6" pine (canopy)
- 4 each ¼"-diameter x 2"-long dowels
- ⅝"-long brads (optional for stack cutting)
- Wood glue
- Temporary bond spray adhesive
- Craft paint: glacier blue, blue heaven, liberty blue, black, metallic silver
- Clear finish

Tools:
- #7 reverse-tooth blades or blades of choice
- Drill press with ¼"-diameter brad-point bit & 9⁄32"-diameter drill bit
- Belt sander and/or sandpaper
- School pencil sharpener

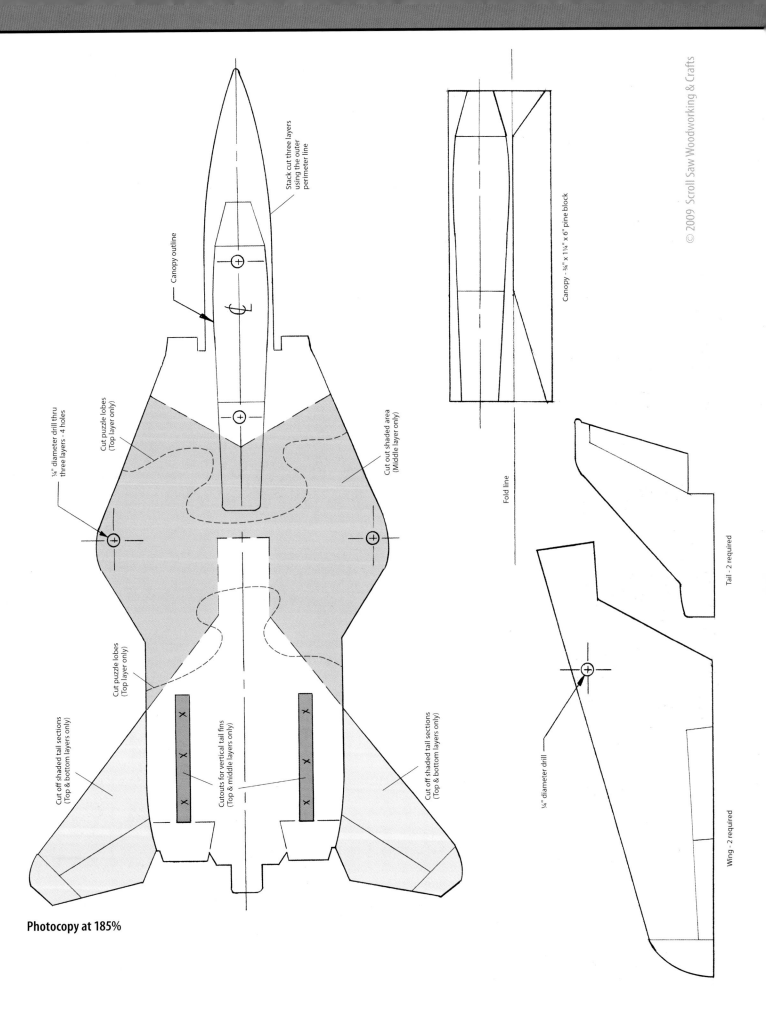

Canopy outline

Stack cut three layers using the outer perimeter line

¼" diameter drill thru three layers - 4 holes

Cut puzzle lobes (Top layer only)

Cut out shaded area (Middle layer only)

Cut puzzle lobes (Top layer only)

Cut off shaded tail sections (Top & bottom layers only)

Cutouts for vertical tail fins (Top & middle layers only)

Cut off shaded tail sections (Top & bottom layers only)

Canopy - ¾" x 1¼" x 6" pine block

Fold line

Tail - 2 required

¼" diameter drill

Wing - 2 required

Photocopy at 185%

Woodimal® Lion

Children always love puzzles and adults will appreciate the subtle humor in the Woodimal lion design.

Scroll this whimsical lion puzzle in two hours or less

By James W. Sweet

Puzzles are always popular, but why do an ordinary puzzle when you can do a Woodimal?

Woodimals are puzzles that are shaped like and spell out the name of the animal, fish, bird, or insect they represent. They are designed as stand alone puzzles and typically take from an hour to an hour and forty-five minutes to complete.

To get started, make several copies of the pattern. Cut your wood to size (for easy handling) and sand both sides of the boards. Then, attach the pattern to the wood using the spray adhesive.

Check to make sure your saw blade is square to the table; otherwise, the puzzle pieces won't go together properly.

Step 1: Begin cutting. Start cutting at the bottom of the rear leg. Scroll saw up the back of the leg, separating the tail from the body. Continue cutting along the back and around the head, leaving excess on the inside of the letter *N* and in the area of the mane. Then, cut down the front of the forward leg. Cut out the area between the front and rear leg. After scroll sawing the outline, cut between the letters.

Step 2: Drill blade entry holes. Drill a ⅛"-diameter blade entry hole in the letter *O*, insert your blade through the hole, and cut out the center of the letter.

Step 3: Make the final body cuts. Finish cutting out the tail. Make your final cuts on the mane and on the inside of the letter *N* to give a ragged appearance.

STANDING THE PUZZLE UP   TIP

Lay the pieces flat on a piece of plywood to assemble them. Then, sit the Woodimal upright.

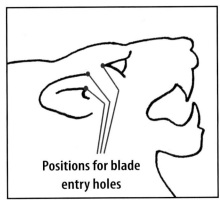

Positions for blade entry holes

Step 4: Drill holes for the facial features. Drill the blade entry holes for the facial features (eye and two ear details) using the #60 drill bit. Insert your blade and complete the inside cuts.

Step 5: Remove the pattern. Lightly sand each piece with 180-grit sandpaper to remove any residue, rough edges, and sharp corners.

Step 6: Clean up the base. Use sandpaper. Rout the edges with the ¼"-diameter round off or ogee router bit.

Finishing

Step 1: Stain. Pour the selected stain into an old cake pan or shallow container and put your puzzle pieces and base into the stain.

Step 2: Drain the pieces. Remove the pieces from the container and place them on an old newspaper, allowing them to drain before wiping off excess stain.

Step 3: Wipe the stain. Before the pieces are completely dry, wipe them with a paper towel or a rag to remove any drip marks.

Step 4: Transfer details. After the parts are completely dry, assemble the puzzle and transfer details onto it using white carbon paper and a stylus.

Photocopy at 195%

Step 5: Continue detailing. Using a #0 or #1 liner brush and black acrylic paint or a woodburner, add the line to show the second rear leg (marked with a dotted line on the pattern). You can also extend the mane down across the front leg if desired.

Step 6: Attach the base. Drill the ⅛"-diameter dowel hole in the bottom of the rear foot and a matching hole in the base as indicated on the pattern. Install the dowel and mount the puzzle on the base.

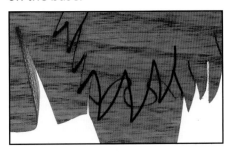

Optional Mane Detail
You can use a #0 or #1 liner brush and black acrylic paint or a woodburner to add details to the bottom of the mane (where the leg piece attaches). Freehand draw the details using a sharp pencil and paint or burn over your lines.

Materials & Tools

Materials:
• ¾"–⅞" x 6½" x 10" for lion (I prefer oak)
• ¾"–⅞" x 2" x 8" for base (I prefer oak)
• ⅛"-diameter dowel rod, ¾" long
• Minwax Golden Oak Stain or stain of choice
• Black acrylic paint (optional)
• Temporary bond spray adhesive

Tools:
• #5 blades of choice
• #60 drill bit
• ⅛"-diameter drill bit
• Drill motor or drill press
• Router
• ¼" round off or ogee router bits
• #0 or #1 liner brush (optional)
• Stylus and carbon paper for transferring details from pattern
• Woodburner (optional)
• Sandpaper, 180 grit
• Shallow container
• Rag

Freestanding Animal Puzzles

Interlocking puzzles have masculine and feminine themes

By Judy and Dave Peterson

You're sure to find the perfect design for each child on your list with these fun animal designs. Choose the noble unicorn or beautiful butterfly for the young women. Opt for the fierce shark or woolly mammoth for the young men on your list.

These puzzles are cut from hardwood, but can be cut in pine or plywood and finished with nontoxic paint. Pay careful attention to the grain direction arrows when transferring the pattern to the blank. You can cut the pieces in any order, but be sure to leave enough wood to hold on to as you cut the smaller pieces. After sanding the pieces, round the edges with a flap sander to soften the look and

remove any fuzzies. Dunk the pieces in natural-colored Danish oil and allow them to dry thoroughly.

If you are making the puzzles for children who may put the pieces in their mouths, use a food-safe finish, such as pure tung oil, or allow the Danish oil to dry according to the manufacturer's instructions. (Most brands suggest a drying time of several weeks).

Photocopy at 100%

Wood grain

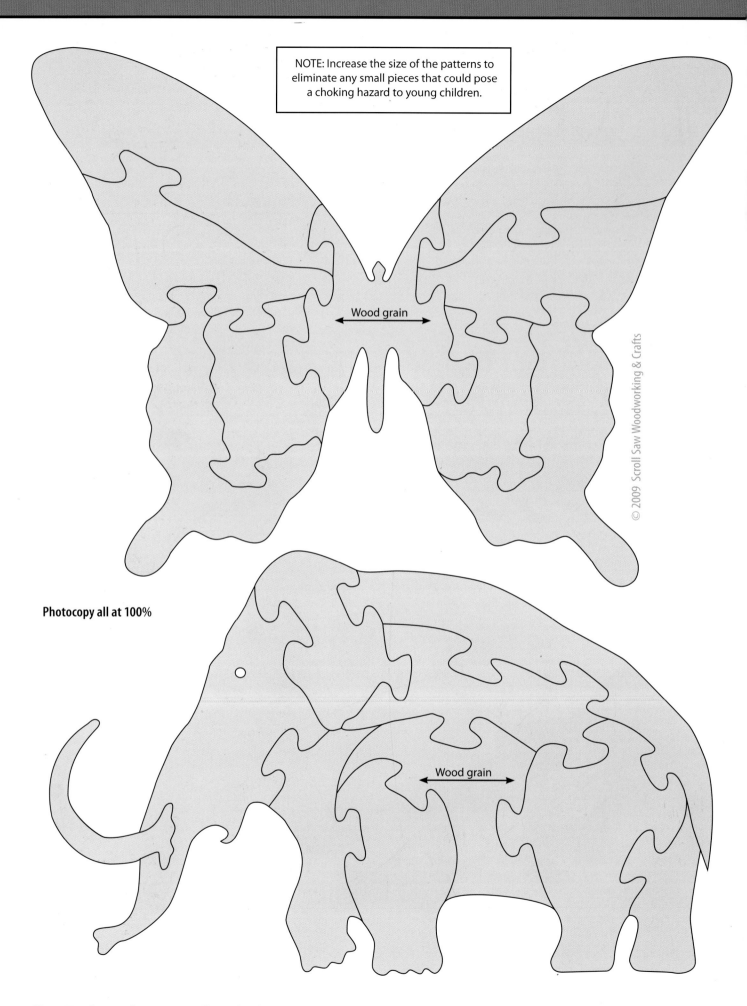

NOTE: Increase the size of the patterns to eliminate any small pieces that could pose a choking hazard to young children.

Wood grain

© 2009 Scroll Saw Woodworking & Crafts

Photocopy all at 100%

Wood grain

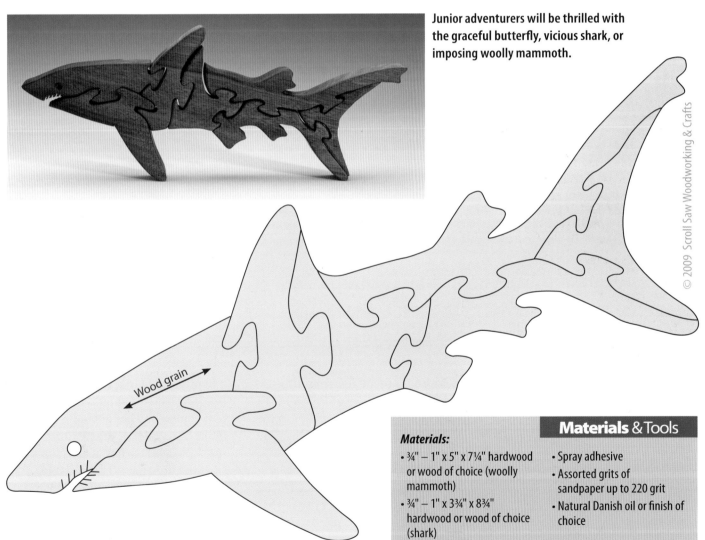

Junior adventurers will be thrilled with the graceful butterfly, vicious shark, or imposing woolly mammoth.

Wood grain

Materials & Tools

Materials:

- ¾" – 1" x 5" x 7¼" hardwood or wood of choice (woolly mammoth)
- ¾" – 1" x 3¾" x 8¾" hardwood or wood of choice (shark)
- ¾" – 1" x 6¼" x 6¼" hardwood or wood of choice (unicorn)
- ¾" – 1" x 6" x 7¾" hardwood or wood of choice (butterfly)

- Spray adhesive
- Assorted grits of sandpaper up to 220 grit
- Natural Danish oil or finish of choice

Tools:

- #5 reverse-tooth blades or blades of choice
- Flap sander

Jonah and the Whale Puzzle

Compound-cut this clever key chain puzzle

By Carl Hird-Rutter

As a child, I recall learning the Sunday school story of Jonah in the belly of a whale—kind of a gloomy place to be, unless you have a scroll saw and some wood!

I was demonstrating the saw at our local fair, and I came up with a fun key chain pattern. It is easy to cut, small enough to use as a key chain, and a fun puzzle to take apart and re-assemble.

Start by making a zero-clearance insert for your saw. The pieces you are going to cut will be too small for a regular table insert. I use low-tack masking tape; if you do not want to use tape on the table of the saw, make a wooden or plastic insert, or use a piece of cardboard. Make sure the table is set at 90°. If the table is off even slightly, you will have problems assembling the puzzle. I have had several of these puzzles broken because people try to force the pieces together.

Step 1: Attach the pattern to the blank. Fold the pattern on the dotted line and spray with temporary bond spray adhesive. Align the fold with the corner of the block and press the pattern down on the wood.

Step 2: Cut the puzzle lobes on the first side. I use a #3 skip-tooth blade. It has a thinner kerf and allows the puzzle to lock together much tighter than a thicker blade. Cut only the puzzle lobes, not the perimeter of the whale's body at this point.

Step 3: Cut out the lobes on the opposite side. Tape the first cut in place. Turn the block so the other side of the pattern is facing up and cut out the next level.

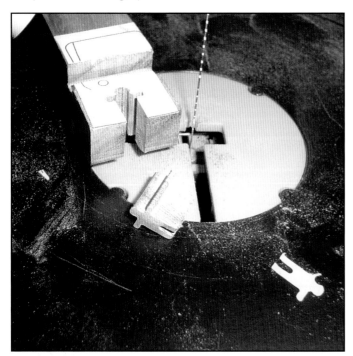

▲ **Step 4: Attach the second pattern to the front block.** The shaded line indicates the recess of the lobe. It is best to have some excess wood in front of the whale's head. This helps keep the piece flat while you are cutting out the profile of Jonah. An alternative is to place shims underneath the lobe. Once you have his profile cut, slice one or two off like gingerbread men.

▲ **Step 5: Cut out the shape of the whale.** Re-assemble the puzzle and tape it together with masking tape or clear packing tape. Cut the top of the whale's body, then retape the block and cut the profile. Finish with the veining cut for the mouth.

Step 6: Drill a 1/16" hole for the eye. Insert a bamboo skewer, a dowel, or a round toothpick to lock the puzzle together. If the hole is too small, chuck the toothpick into an electric drill and sand it down.

Step 7: Apply a wax finish. Finishing with varnish may make it hard to reassemble. Attach an eyehook and a keychain ring to the front of the whale's head.

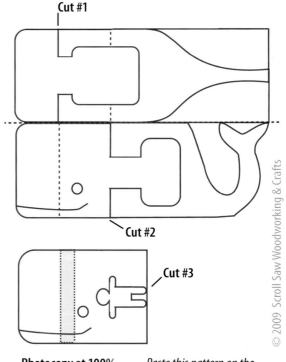

Cut #1

Cut #2

Cut #3

© 2009 Scroll Saw Woodworking & Crafts

Photocopy at 100%   *Paste this pattern on the front of the whale after the second cut has been made.*

Materials & Tools

Materials:
- 1" x 1" x 6" hardwood of choice
- Bamboo skewer or round toothpick
- Temporary bond spray adhesive
- Wax finish
- Assorted grits of sandpaper
- Eyehook and keychain ring (optional)

Tools:
- #3 skip-tooth blades or blades of choice
- Drill with 1/16"-diameter drill bit

Woodimal® Moose

This educational puzzle captures the majestic nature of the moose

By James W. Sweet

Woodimals are not only good conversation pieces; they are a great learning tool for children. The moose is another in this series of puzzles designed to "stand alone." These puzzles may also be made as inlays by laying them flat within a frame surrounded by free-form puzzle pieces.

The moose is the largest member of the deer family, but it doesn't look like its much smaller relatives. It has a long face and a muzzle that hangs loosely over its chin. The large fold of skin that dangles from its chin is called a "bell." The antlers are not like those of a deer. They are solid and may have a span of over 6' with as many as 40 points. The bull may measure as much as 7' at the shoulder with a weight of more than 1,800 pounds. For our purposes, we will show the project as a stand alone puzzle.

Step 1: Prepare to cut. Trim the blank to size for easy handling, and transfer the pattern to the wood, using your method of choice. Ensure that the scroll saw table is square to the blade using a small square or your method of choice.

Step 2: Drill blade entry holes. Use a ⅛"-diameter drill bit for the O's and a #60 drill bit for the inside-line cuts. If you do not want to make inside cuts, you can transfer the details from the pattern to your puzzle piece and use acrylic paint or a woodburner to add the details.

Step 3: Cut out the moose's outline. Begin scrolling from the bottom of the front or rear leg. Continue around the outside of the puzzle, separating the antlers from the head as you scroll the outline. Lay the antlers aside and finish scrolling them separately. Allow excess around the bell on the neck so you can come back and give it a ragged appearance. When the outline is complete, cut the area between the front and rear legs. Then, cut out the area between each pair of legs. If necessary, you can sand the bottom of the feet to ensure they are all the same length.

Step 4: Cut out the letters. Separate the letters in any sequence you choose.

Step 5: Complete scrolling the outside of the antlers.

Step 6: Cut the notches on the bell. You want to give it a ragged appearance.

Step 7: Make the inside cuts. Insert your blade through the blade entry holes in the O's. Follow the same procedure to make the other interior cuts. If you do not want to make inside-line cuts, you can use acrylic paints or a woodburner to add the details.

Step 8: Sand the pieces. Remove the pattern, and lightly sand each piece with 180-grit sandpaper to remove any adhesive residue, rough edges, or sharp corners.

Step 9: Make the base. Cut the base to its final dimensions. Shape the edges of the base, using a ¼"-diameter round-off or ogee router bit.

Step 10: Drill the ⅛"-diameter hole in the bottom of the foot. Drill a matching hole in the base where indicated on the pattern. This hole is for the dowel that lets the moose stand upright (see Step 13).

Step 11: Stain the pieces. Pour the selected stain into an old cake pan or shallow container, and put your puzzle pieces and base into the stain. Remove the pieces from the container and place them onto an old newspaper. Allow them to drain before wiping off the excess stain. Before the pieces are completely dry, wipe them with a paper towel or a rag to remove any drip marks.

Step 12 (optional): Add the details to the puzzle. Assemble the puzzle and transfer any necessary details using the white carbon paper and a stylus. Using a sponge brush and a #0 or #1 liner brush, apply the acrylic paints as follows: antlers—tan; ear, eye, nostril, and lines on antlers—black (if you did not make inside-line cuts).

Step 13: Install the ⅛"-diameter dowel in the previously drilled hole. Mount the completed puzzle onto the base.

Materials & Tools

Materials:
- ¾"–⅞" x 11" x 9" hardwood of choice (moose)
- ¾"–⅞" x 2" x 7" hardwood of choice (base)
- ⅛"-diameter x ¾"-long dowel rod
- Sandpaper, 180 grit
- Minwax Golden Oak Stain or your stain of choice
- Acrylic paints in black and tan (optional)
- Spray adhesive of choice

Tools:
- #5 blades of choice
- #60 drill bit
- ⅛"-diameter drill bit

- Drill motor or drill press
- Router with ¼"-diameter round-off or ogee router bit
- #0 or #1 liner brush (optional)
- Stylus and white carbon paper for transferring details from pattern (optional)
- Woodburner (optional)
- Shallow container
- Rag

NOTE: A belt sander with an attached disc sander and a planer are always helpful when working with wood.

Drill ⅛"-diameter dowel hole

Photocopy at 125%

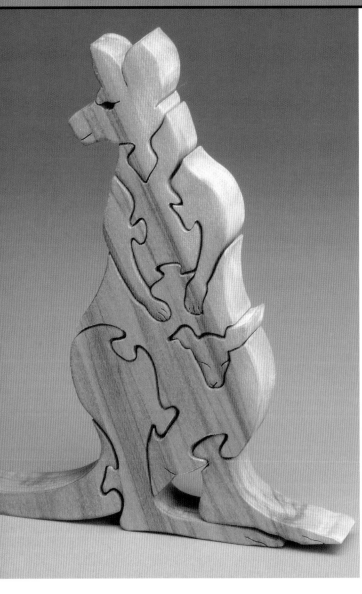

Kangaroo Puzzle

Create this beautiful Down Under duo

By Judy and Dave Peterson

Materials &Tools

Materials:
- ¾"–1" x 8" x 9" hardwood or wood of choice
- Clear packaging tape
- Clear, outdoor Danish oil with UV blocker or finish of choice
- Spray adhesive
- Assorted grits of sandpaper up to 220 grit

Tools:
- #7 reverse-tooth blades or blades of choice
- Flap sander (optional)
- Paintbrush or rag

Several folks requested a kangaroo puzzle, and I eventually came up with this version. The original design had more pieces, and the mother kangaroo was facing forward. Sales of the puzzle were weak, so I tweaked the pattern to include fewer pieces. This reduced the time it takes to cut the pattern, allowing me to lower the price, and sales picked up.

The kangaroo puzzle does contain small pieces that present a choking hazard for children under three. Take care to keep this puzzle out of the reach of small children.

© 2009 Scroll Saw Woodworking & Crafts

Photocopy at 120%

Master Puzzles

In this section, master puzzle makers can find not only puzzles to sharpen their skills, but also inspiration for making their own designs. In addition to the instructions and patterns, the following pages contain hints, tips, and galleries of work to help you improve your techniques.

Layered Marquetry Puzzles by
Steve Malavolta, page 74.

Layered Marquetry Puzzles

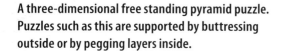

A challenge to create and a greater challenge to assemble

By Steve Malavolta
Photography by Pat Berrett

A set of two matched puzzles with interchangeable pieces. The puzzles are made of contrasting wood, but cut so you can swap pieces back and forth between the two.

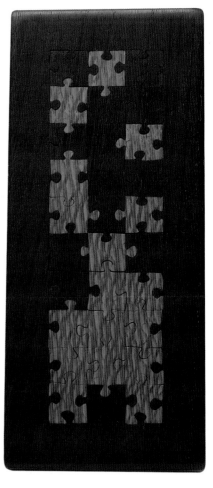

A three-dimensional free standing pyramid puzzle. Puzzles such as this are supported by buttressing outside or by pegging layers inside.

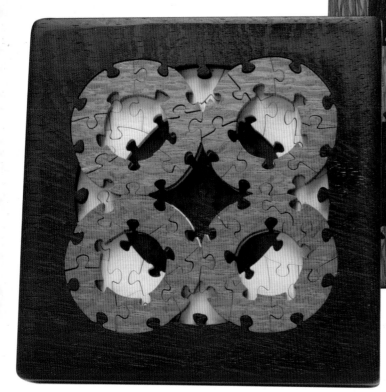

One of Steve's more challenging puzzles is the layered ring puzzle. In addition to having the layers, the illusion of negative space makes the puzzles even harder to solve.

Puzzle-Making Philosophy

My 26-year interest in woodworking has a lot to do with wood itself. Wood contains workable qualities—variations of color, shapability, and textile qualities when finished—that compliment the pieces I make.

My puzzles have evolved over the years. The earlier pieces were only nicely colored and figured slabs of wood, cut into somewhat undefined pieces and then framed out. Currently, I am incorporating my inlay abilities in a style similar to intarsia and creating landscapes, abstracts, and 3-D architectural puzzles.

All of my woods are hand-picked for consistency of grain, coloration, and figuration. These aspects lead me, the designer, into the creation of the individual piece. The inlay work and cutting is done on a scroll saw with a jeweler's blade.

I have always incorporated function into my artwork, and the puzzles are very important to me because they allow people to experience both visual gratification and tactile enjoyment. Each puzzle is made with the intent to be played, creating both entertainment and intellectual challenges.

My goal as a woodworker is to present my puzzles as enjoyable, playable, heirloom-quality artwork. I recommend you practice some of these woodworking techniques and enjoy the pleasures that the process of creating and the use of the finished piece returns to you.

Steve uses his marquetry techniques to create a landscape scene puzzle. He uses different woods for different colors and embellishes the work with sterling silver and small stones.

This puzzle uses Steve's layering technique to simulate flames.

Using his layering technique, Steve gives a sense of movement to his puzzles. These layers really increase the difficulty of his puzzles.

Alternating layers of contrasting woods increases the beauty and difficulty of this puzzle.

Steve used the marquetry techniques to create a different landscape scene.

Challenging Puzzles

One of the concerns I have in creating a puzzle is the challenge. My puzzles range from single layer entertainment to multi-layered, complicated sculptural challenges.

One of the initial challenges comes from the fact that all the pieces are freehand cut, creating odd and irregular-shaped pieces. The next challenge comes from the woods I work with—all naturally colored and finished hardwoods. Additionally, all pieces are finished on both sides, so the puzzle solver needs to determine which is right side up before deciding where the piece belongs. There is no flipping all the cardboard sides down and all the picture sides up, as you do with the stamped-out picture puzzles. I also cut lobes and sockets into the frames of the puzzles, so that way there are no straight edges or definable corner pieces.

If all of this isn't enough, many of my style puzzles are layered—a concept quite unique to my puzzles. The challenge is compounded when the various layers are made of the same wood, making it possible to assemble part of a layer in the wrong level of the frame. Most people only discover this as they progress further into the puzzle assembly.

Another of Steve's inlay-style puzzles, this one is also embellished with sterling silver wire.

One of my more challenging designs is a puzzle I called the "Layered Rings." It incorporates all the previous challenges plus the illusion of negative space. The image created is similar to layers of gears or cogs. Every piece and all of the frame cuts have lobes and sockets cut into them, but not every piece is intended to connect into a matching cut, thereby further confusing the matter. This puzzle is recommended only for the serious puzzler.

I also create one-of-a-kind and limited edition sculptural puzzles. These puzzles are often architectural in form, stacking layers of pieces, creating three-dimensional sculptures mounted onto a base and often housed under a glass case. These puzzles are frequently frameless and held together by buttressing and/or fixed pegging from layer to layer.

The layered rings add to the difficulty to these puzzles because it is possible to assemble one of the rings out of order.

Steve Shares His Puzzle-Making Techniques

In-Process Photos by Valerie Gooch

I started my 24-year career as a self-taught woodworker making lap dulcimers and guitars, which incorporated inlay, and I've spent much time producing hand-cut wooden jigsaw puzzles. Because holiday gift-making is a tradition of mine, I made a stand-up serpent puzzle for my nephew. This was the start of a new career and what I sometimes consider an obsession.

Wood Selection and Preparation

Making my puzzles starts with the wood selection. I usually use nicely figured, consistently dense, and colorful woods. I buy most pieces in 4/4 to 8/4 stock and re-saw them to approximately 5⁄16" thick using a Delta 14" band saw fitted with a height extension. The extension allows me to re-saw stock up to 12" high. At the speed my saw is running, I have found a ½" 4-hook tooth blade works best.

Because of the thinness of my finished woods, density and tightness of grain are important. Once cut into puzzle pieces, woods with irregular density, such as oak, make for weak spots, increasing the possibility of breakage. Softer woods and checked, or cracked, woods also have breakage problems.

Re-saw and sand the four pieces of wood to 5/32"-thick.

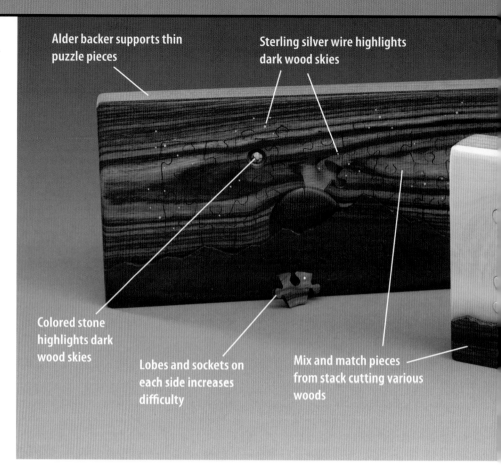

Alder backer supports thin puzzle pieces

Sterling silver wire highlights dark wood skies

Colored stone highlights dark wood skies

Lobes and sockets on each side increases difficulty

Mix and match pieces from stack cutting various woods

Once re-sawn, I finish sand the material on a 36" dual drum sander at my shop or rent time on a 54" overhead belt sander, depending on the amount of wood I need surfaced. The 5⁄16"-thick stock is reduced to 5⁄32"-thick and finished with 220-grit sandpaper. Thickness planers can do the job, but because of the thinness of the wood, chipping can occur, especially with denser, figured grains. A backing board helps in these cases. Alternately, you can purchase pre-finished thinner stock from some wood suppliers.

Tools and Equipment

Although I use a whole shop worth of tools to create a puzzle from start to finish, the scroll saw is my main tool and the one worth offering some advice on. Most reciprocating scroll saws do the job, and most manufacturers offer very useable and affordable choices. I currently use a Delta Variable Speed C Arm

model with some personalized modifications. I also like many of the parallelogram models.

For me, variable speed adjustment is helpful because I work from 600 strokes per minute to 1400 strokes per minute, depending on the thickness and density of the wood, teeth per inch on the blade, and type of control I need.

Another important feature on a saw is a quick-change blade setup. Because most blades last me an average of only ten minutes, I prefer blade clamps that tighten by an Allen wrench or a thumbscrew.

Also, pay attention to your blade tension. A blade that is too tight will break prematurely. One that is too loose will give a beveled cut, producing pieces that will not slide in and out of each other freely. Once you find the proper tension of the blades in your saw, pluck them like a guitar string. Remembering the notes for each size blade will help give you the correct tension for your next blade installation.

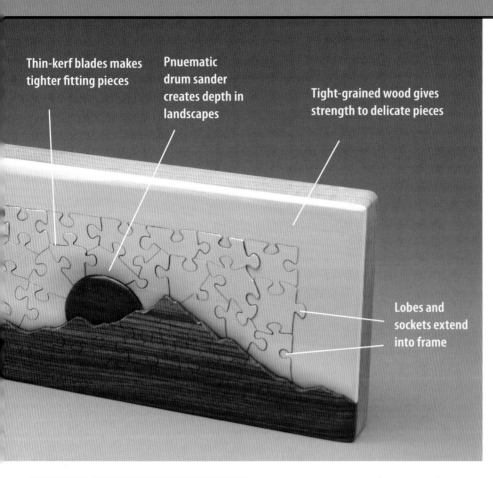

Thin-kerf blades makes tighter fitting pieces

Pnuematic drum sander creates depth in landscapes

Tight-grained wood gives strength to delicate pieces

Lobes and sockets extend into frame

Now, draw the landscape. Remember, each section of the design will need to be cut into pieces, so don't make these sections too small or delicate. Also, when drawing the landscape design, remember that you will want a border about ¾" to frame the bottom, top, and side edges.

Make each section large enough to accommodate the landscape and interior pieces. In this puzzle, the sections go right to the outside edge, so a starting hole is not necessary. However, on enclosed shapes, I use a #70 drill bit for the starting hole.

Once the design is drawn, cut it using a 24 tpi blade with a cutting kerf, or blade width, of .011" to produce an identical section in each kind of wood (four sky sections, four planets, and four mountains). You can mix and

Carefully cut along the lines for the landscape.

Keep the blade in the center when pivoting the wood through its curvy path. If it isn't centered, you will stress the blade sideways, either beveling the cut or breaking the blade.

Layout

Each style puzzle has its own process, but I mostly work in a manner very similar to marquetry.

Start by choosing up to 4 pieces of different colored wood and cut them to equal length and width. As an example, I will focus on setting up a single layer landscape puzzle. Once the four pieces of wood are cut, position them so the more

exciting section of grain is always in the upper section and facing up. This position will orient the grain in the sky area of the drawing.

Next, stack them, with the lightest colored piece on top, so the landscape sketch is easily seen. Place a small dab of quick set epoxy on each of the four corners and clamp until dry. This temporarily holds the blanks together while you draw and make the inlay cuts.

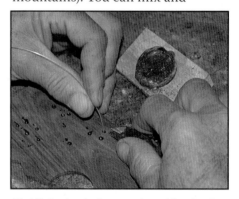

Highlight the darker wood used for the sky scenes using sterling silver wire. Drill tiny holes and glue the wire in.

Using the different cut-out elements, mix and match to make four different puzzles.

Using a pneumatic drum sander, sand the edges of the sections of your choice down to create a relief effect.

match, still ending up with four puzzle blanks, as in our original stack of wood.

At this time, I often add highlights. Sterling silver wire works great for stars in the darker sky blanks. Start by drilling holes for two different gauge wire. Then, dip the silver wire in CA glue before inserting it into the hole and cutting it off. Make sure that it is protruding just a bit on both the top and bottom of the blank. Once the glue is dry, put the blank on a belt sander and smooth the silver down to the wood's surface.

I also highlight by drilling a cupped hole with a burring bit just shy of the depth of the wood. Later, I glue a half-dome stone in the hole for a moon.

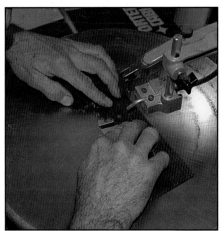

Using a very fine blade, cut out each of the puzzle pieces leaving a lobe or a socket on each side of the piece.

Making Delicate Cuts

Since the blades I use are so fine, I want to eliminate as much stress on the blade as possible. One way is to check what I call the "parallel stroke" of the saw by viewing the blade from the front—the top and bottom clamping point should be perfectly aligned. To check it, move the blade to the up position, then place a flat piece of material on the cutting table just against the blade. Slowly move the blade to the lowest position of its stroke; it should not move any further away or closer to your placed material. If there is any movement from side to side, this will cause extra friction on the blade, shortening its life. Some older saws have an adjustment for this on the back portion of the upper frame. Newer saws usually don't have any sort of adjustment, so some shimming at the blade clamps might be necessary.

Additionally, I do some relief work to the sky and planet. Relief sanding adds depth, and I've found that the best way to sand is to hold the section at about a 15° angle against the idle pulley of a belt sander fitted with a 60-grit belt. Bevel into the edge to approximately half of its thickness. Then, finish sand these edges on a 3" pneumatic drum sander with 220-grit paper.

Piece Cutting and Finishing

After years of practice, planning and cutting the puzzles is spontaneous for me—I plan the pieces as I cut. However, when you start out, it's a good idea to draw the pieces ahead of time.

First, draw a pencil line border approximately 1" in from the outside edges. Anything inside this border will be puzzle pieces. Then, switch to a 31-tpi blade with a kerf of .008". This finer blade keeps any looseness from the kerf to a minimum. Because of the thin blade, cut single sections at a time. Stack cutting seems to create too much bevel

in the cut, preventing the pieces from fitting properly. As I cut along the line marking the border of the frame, I include a lobe or socket for each adjoining puzzle piece—eliminating straight edge pieces and helping tighten the puzzle by locking it all to the frame.

To further limit the amount of looseness from the kerf, make sure each side of each piece has a lobe and socket connection. Another technique that helps with looseness is to occasionally join two adjacent pieces to a single side of another piece. Do this every fifth piece or so.

Lobes and Sockets

Lobes and sockets are the mirror images of each other—the negative and positive portions of the cuts you make. My pieces are cut in a very traditional style, making sure there is at least one lobe and socket on every side. The lobe needs to be a well-defined cut, similar to the head and neck area of the human body. The neck needs to be narrower than the head but wide enough to avoid becoming a weak spot. This well-defined area of the piece is what creates a good locking puzzle piece. The size of the pieces is not too important, but remember that you do not want pieces to be so small or delicate that they break during play. My pieces average approximately ¾" square.

Because of the irregular shape of the sections in the designs, freehand piece cutting is almost mandatory. I find it easier to cut pieces that are not drawn. However, as I am cutting, I plan at least four pieces in advance.

If you still need to draw the pieces in advance, try using a grid system to give yourself a guideline. The grid system often used in puzzles can be modified to work within the irregular shaped sections.

Assembly

As I cut the pieces, usually in groups of four or five, I end up in a dead end. Then, I stop the saw and transfer them from the saw to a piece of newsprint, making sure to keep the pieces in order.

Once the puzzle is completely cut, place the frame sections around it and transport it to the sanding table. Hand sand the top and bottom with a rubber sanding block fitted with 220-grit paper. Then, hand rub them with 00 steel wool to burnish them to an even finer finish, making sure that all the burring and pencil marks are removed. To

Sand the puzzle first with a belt sander and then with a pneumatic drum sander to soften the edges.

turn the puzzle over, use a manila envelope—slide the puzzle off the newsprint into the manila envelope, then butt it up to the fold, close the envelope, and flip it over.

Most of my puzzles are backed with 4/4 alder. Cut a piece slightly larger than the puzzle itself. Glue the frame sections onto the alder backing using PVA glue. Once dry, trim and square the frame using a table saw and radial arm saw. Then, finish sand these frames on a belt sander and soften the edges on a 6" pneumatic drum sander, each time working with a finer grit, ending up around 220 grit.

Glue the puzzle frame to whatever board you are using to back it.

I sign, date, and list the woods on the back of each puzzle, using a Foredom Flexshaft with an etching burr.

Finishing

For the first finish, brush on a coat of Watco Natural Oil and wait until it begins to thicken before wiping off the excess. Do both sides of the pieces using another manila envelope to flip the puzzle. I usually wait 24 hours between each oiling.

Next, lightly hand rub the puzzle with tung oil. Start with the back of the pieces and wait an hour or so before wiping off the excess. Wait 24 hours before sliding the puzzle pieces into the already oiled and dry frame. Then, apply tung oil to the assembled puzzle and frame. Again, wait an hour or so before wiping off the excess.

After another 24 hours, apply a light coat of wax, buffing to a finish after it dries.

Photocopy at 110%

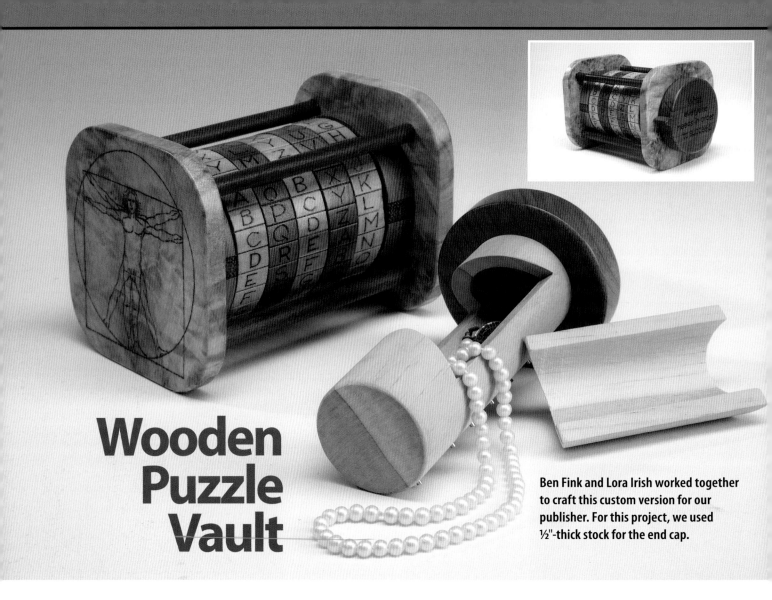

Wooden Puzzle Vault

Ben Fink and Lora Irish worked together to craft this custom version for our publisher. For this project, we used ½"-thick stock for the end cap.

Clever design will keep them guessing

By Donald Horgan
Process photos by Dennis Horgan

While reading *The DaVinci Code* by Dan Brown, I was intrigued by the description of what he called a "Cryptex," or vault protected by a combination lock. After reading the passage describing the cryptex, I knew I had to design one in wood. The project is actually quite simple and can be put together in a weekend with tools most woodworkers have.

I have been a police officer for 16 years and have used woodworking as the ultimate stress reliever. This project combines my love of reading, a life of law enforcement, and my passion for woodworking.

I worked my way through several prototypes and was excited to try out the finished product on my family and friends. The reactions were priceless! With each new vault, my children bug me to give them "just the first letter." My colleagues try to figure out a mechanical way around the lock! With a five-dial vault, using all 26 letters, there are 11,881,376 possible combinations! It is a great conversational piece and could be used to conceal a small gift for a special birthday or anniversary.

To get started building your own vault, attach the pattern for the seven rings to the blank, using spray adhesive. Cover the pattern with clear packaging tape. The side with the pattern attached will be called Side A. The opposite side will be called Side B.

1 **Drill one side of the rings.** Drill a ⅟₁₆"-diameter hole through the center of each ring so you can locate the center from either side. Be careful, the center is important to the smooth working of the vault. Using a 1⅞"-diameter Forstner bit, drill ¼" deep on six of the rings. The seventh undrilled ring will become the bottom ring.

2 **Drill the holes in Side B.** Turn the material over. You should be able to see the center hole. Use this as a reference, and drill a 1⅝"-diameter hole ¼" deep. Do not drill the first ring, as this will become the top ring, and do not drill the bottom ring. Then, drill a 1⅜"-diameter hole through the center of all seven rings. To reduce tearout, drill partway through from each side.

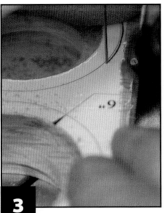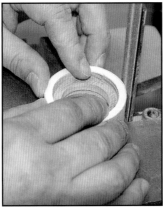

3 **Cut out each of the rings.** Your five main rings will have a hollow core with a 1⅞"-diameter opening on the A side, a 1⅝"-diameter opening on the B side, and a 1⅜"-diameter lip in the center. I use a #7 blade to cut the perimeter of the rings. Cut ⅟₁₆" outside the line and sand to the line with a belt or disk sander.

4 **Add a rabbet around each ring.** With Side A facing up on a router table, use a ¼"-radius rabbeting bit to cut a ¼" x ¼" rabbet around each ring. Use a push block to hold the ring. Your fingers will be close to the bit. This rabbet allows the rings to nest inside of each other.

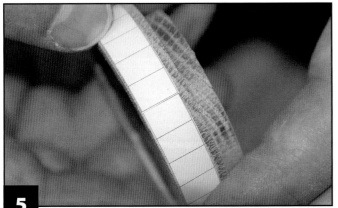

5 **Cut out and attach the letter dial marking templates to the five interior rings.** If you cut precise rings, the templates will wrap around the rings, line up end to end, and divide the ring into 26 equal sections. If the rings are not the correct circumference, cut a little away from the lines on each space in the next step to tweak the difference over several spaces.

6 **Define the letter spaces and cut the keyway.** Use a #7 or finer blade to score the spaces for the letters. Cut one notch on the interior of the ring, corresponding to a letter space on the outer perimeter. These notches become the keyway, allowing you to remove the vault. Randomize the notch locations with respect to the grain, so the grain pattern can't be used to solve the code.

7 **Mark the end rings.** Stack a letter ring next to the end rings. Transfer lines for one letter space and score the lines on your saw. Cut the interior notch on the top ring, matching the scored lines. On the bottom ring, center a notch between the scored lines, just wide enough for a nail, to prevent wiggling of the vault.

8 **Drill the hole in the center compartment.** The interior compartment is made from a 1⅜"-diameter dowel. Cut the dowel to a length of 4⅜". Mark the center on one end. Drill a ⅞"-diameter hole 3⅜"-deep. Be sure to keep the hole square to the dowel. Clamp the dowel, and use a drill press.

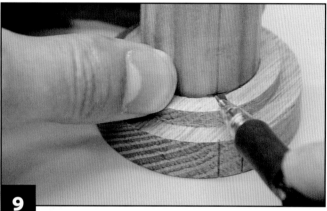

9 **Mark the location of the locking pins.** Mark a line the length of the dowel. Place the dowel (with the opening on top) in the bottom ring. Mark the top of the ring on the line. Add the first ring and mark the top on the dowel line. Use the same method to mark the location of the next three rings. This removes any discrepancies that may prevent the rings from turning.

10 **Insert the pins.** Mark ⅜" below the first mark on the dowel. This will house the pin that fits into the slot on the bottom ring. Clip both ends off of a 3d finish nail and use it to drill a hole at the mark you just made and at each of the four marks for the letter dials. Clip the points off of five more nails, and glue them in place with CA glue. Cut the nails to a ⅛" height.

11 **Cut the access door.** Put the dowel inside the rings and mark the location of the top of the seventh ring. Cut the door just below the mark, on the opposite side of the pins. An angled cut on the ends will help keep the door closed. Drill a 1⅜"-diameter x ⅜"-deep hole in the end cap, then cut the perimeter.

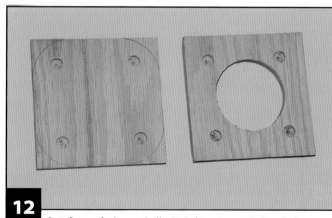

12 **Cut the end pieces.** Drill a 5/16"-diameter x ⅛"-deep hole in the corners of both framework ends as shown on the pattern. Cut the rounded corners and drill a 1⅞" hole through the center of one piece. Sand the edges or round them over on the router table. Round the edges of the end cap with a ⅛"-radius round-over bit.

13 **Cut the dowel supports.** Measure the total height of the seven rings stacked one on top of another. It should be close to 3½". Add twice the actual depth of the ⁵⁄₁₆"-diameter holes in the end caps, and an additional ¹⁄₁₆". This gives enough room for the rings to turn easily. Cut four ⁵⁄₁₆"-diameter dowels to this length. Dry fit all the pieces together including the end cap and dowel.

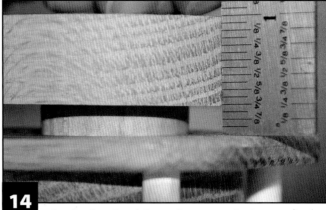

14 **Trim the dowel and determine your code.** Measure the space between the frame and the end cap. Trim that much minus ¹⁄₃₂" from the open end of the dowel so the end cap clears the frame. Write the code letters in the spaces over each notch on the letter dials and continue the alphabet from those letters. Darken the single spaces on the two end rings.

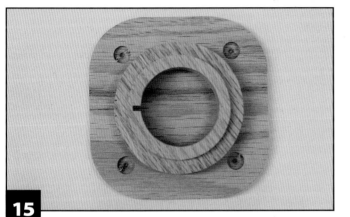

15 **Assemble the cryptex.** Glue the bottom ring in the middle of the solid framework end, with the notch pointing to the center of one side. Glue the top ring into the hollow framework end, aligning the notch in the center to match the bottom. Keep the grain running the same direction on the ends and the end cap.

16 **Glue the final pieces in place.** Glue the support dowels to the bottom, stack the rings in the proper order and glue the top framework in place. Align the pointer on the end cap with the pins on the dowel, and glue it onto the open end of the dowel. Clamp both assemblies and allow to dry. Apply a clear spray finish.

Materials & Tools

Materials:
- ¾" x 5½" x 11" red oak or wood of choice (rings and end cap)
- ¼" x 3½" x 7" wood of choice (framework ends)
- 18" of ⁵⁄₁₆"-diameter dowel
- 5" of 1⅜"-diameter dowel
- 6 each 3d finishing nails
- Spray adhesive
- Clear spray finish
- Wood glue

Tools:
- #7 blades or blades of choice
- Drill press

- ¹⁄₁₆"-diameter twist drill bit
- 1⅞"-, 1⅝"-, and 1⅜"-diameter Forstner bits
- ⁵⁄₁₆"-diameter brad point or Forstner bit
- ⅞"-diameter spade or Forstner bit
- Table saw (optional)
- Miter saw (optional)
- Router or router table with ⅛" and ¼"-radius round-over bits and ¼" rabbeting bit
- A belt or disk sander
- Dremel tool with cut-off wheel or diagonal cutters
- Ultra-fine permanent marker

Making it difficult

The more equidistant the pins are from the bottoms of the rings, the harder it will be to exploit the mechanical weaknesses to solve the code. You can create false mechanical "hints" by creating divots in the bottom side of the inner rings to give the illusion of a pin sliding up into a notch. This is especially effective when placing the divots on vowels, and the letters R, S, T, and L.

Provide a hint that will not give away the answer too quickly. Cryptic rhymes or questions work well.

Don's original cryptex was unlocked with the code word ENJOY.

Neater Letters

Printing neat letters on the round dials can be somewhat of a challenge. With some practice and a steady hand, you can get good results with a fine tip marker or a woodburner.

An alternate method is to add the alphabet with rub-on letters used for scrapbooks. They are available at many craft stores in a variety of fonts and once sealed, the letters are very durable.

EXPLODED DRAWING

A view of the male and female ends of the rotating rings. The notches cut into the inside of the rings make a keyway for the pins to follow.

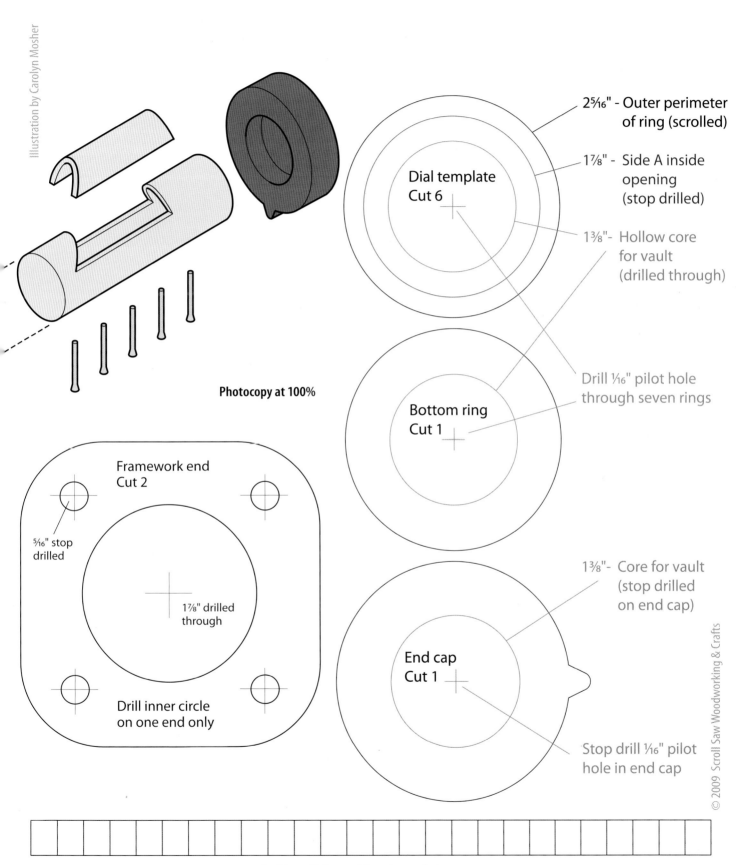

Illustration by Carolyn Mosher

Photocopy at 100%

2⁵⁄₁₆" - Outer perimeter of ring (scrolled)

1⅞" - Side A inside opening (stop drilled)

1⅜"- Hollow core for vault (drilled through)

Dial template
Cut 6

Drill ¹⁄₁₆" pilot hole through seven rings

Bottom ring
Cut 1

Framework end
Cut 2

⁵⁄₁₆" stop drilled

1⅞" drilled through

Drill inner circle on one end only

1⅜"- Core for vault (stop drilled on end cap)

End cap
Cut 1

Stop drill ¹⁄₁₆" pilot hole in end cap

© 2009 Scroll Saw Woodworking & Crafts

Letter dial marking template

Wooly Mammoth Puzzle

Veining lines add detail and a maddening twist

By Bob Betting

The plan is slightly different than the photo of the project. During the cutting it was noted that some minor improvements could be made. These were primarily in the interlocking designs.

Jim Sweet's Woodimals® inspired me to develop my own series of puzzles. Jim's Woodimals are very clever puzzles that utilize letters of the animal's name cut out so that when they are placed together, they form the animal's shape. In my series, Paleo Pets, the animals are extinct, and they are not name puzzles. The twist with my puzzles is that I use texture patterns created by definition cuts—sometimes called veining—to hide where the pieces interlock. In the featured animal in this article, there are only 33 pieces, but it can be maddening to assemble.

Step 1: Preparing to cut. Select your wood. I used poplar; other woods with good grain patterns include red oak, ash, birch, maple, and white oak. Attach a copy of the pattern to your wood using either a temporary bond spray adhesive or a removable glue stick. Glue so that the supporting feet for the puzzle are on the bottom edge of the board. The top edge of the board must be parallel with the bottom edge for drilling the dowel holes.

Step 2: Drilling the holes. Drill ⅛"-diameter holes to the required depth for the dowels. Use a drill press and a plastic triangle or combination square against the board to make sure the holes are being drilled vertically to the base. Drill a ½₂"-diameter access hole in the eye and the opening in the end of the trunk.

Though this puzzle has only 33 interlocking pieces, it's surprisingly difficult to assemble. The more pieces you connect, the harder it is to tell the puzzle pieces from the definition lines.

Step 3: Cutting head details. Cut the trunk opening, the eye, and the connecting definition lines. With a #3 blade, cut the line across the forehead to the remainder of the definition lines around the eye.

Step 4: Cutting the outline. Cut the outline of the puzzle all the way around. Since the outside edge is not critical, I used a #7 double-tooth blade. If you've chosen a wood harder than poplar, you may want to use a #9. With a #4 or #5 blade, cut all of the definition lines that begin on the outside of the puzzle.

Step 5: Cutting the pieces.
Pieces that stick out such as the tusk, trunk, and legs should be cut first. Following lines exactly is not necessary except when cutting the parts of the pieces that actually interlock.

Cut at a 90° angle to the tabletop so the pieces slide apart from both the front and back of the puzzle. Even if your blade is at a 90°, you still might get an arced cut if you feed the wood too fast or cut with a dull blade.

Determine which piece will be the last to cut. Choose a large piece so you have surface to hold onto while cutting. I used a #4 double-tooth blade for cutting the puzzle pieces and the interior definition cuts. A larger blade creates a wider kerf and a looser fit. A smaller blade makes it more difficult to make cuts that are perfectly square with the face of the board, especially hardwoods.

Begin from the outside edge to cut the first puzzle piece. As the cut intersects a branching definition cut, make the definition cut into the puzzle piece you are cutting. Finish cutting out the puzzle piece. Test it to make sure it slides into the rest of the puzzle both from the front and from the back. If it does not, fix the cause before cutting more.

If at any time a piece splits off, you can generally glue it back on. Should any glue get on the puzzle surface, remove the glue with mineral spirits before it completely dries. In the worst case, it will be a split adjacent to the edge of a puzzle piece. It may then be necessary to glue the two puzzle pieces together.

Step 6: Making the definition cuts on the interior pieces. Make the definition cuts that end on the edge of the puzzle. Simply cut to the end, then back the blade out. I don't recommend pivoting the workpiece to make the return cut because it tends to leave a noticeable hole.

Position the assembled puzzle face up and pull off what you can of the pattern from the wood. Use a shop towel to liberally apply paint thinner on any remaining pattern pieces. After the thinner soaks in for about five or so minutes, the paper will be loose. Rub the top of the puzzle with the thinner-soaked rag to remove any remaining glue residue.

Step 7: Rounding the pieces.
Rounding the back side edges allows the pieces to slide into each other more easily. The larger the radii of the roundings and the smoother they are, the easier and less frustrating it will be to put the puzzle together. Round only those portions that fit together. Do not round the edges of the outside of the puzzle. A handheld grinding tool works great, but use what works best for you. Sand the rounded edges with 220-grit sandpaper.

▲ **Step 8: Numbering the puzzle pieces.** To allow the numbers to stand out, I painted a spot on the backs of the pieces with Minwax Polycrylic before staining to limit the amount of stain that would be absorbed.

I used a permanent ink marker to print numbers on the backs of the pieces after the stain had dried. Do not try to mark them prior to staining as the ink will follow the grain lines on many woods. If you choose an oil finish, do the marking after the oil has dried. While the puzzle was assembled face-down, the marking was done with all numbers oriented "up." I started numbering at the head, with adjacent pieces given the next number. A coat of polycrylic ensures that the numbers can't be rubbed off.

Step 9: Staining the pieces. Dip each puzzle piece except the tusk in ebony oil-based stain, remove, wipe, and allow to dry. The stain accents the definition cuts as well as the edges of the pieces. A quick dip gives maximum contrast to the wood grain.

Step 10: Creating the base. Cut the base to a size and from a wood you think attractive. It should not be of thinner material than the puzzle. I used an 11" piece of ¾" x 1" x 3" bird's-eye maple. Drill ⅛"-diameter dowel holes ½" deep, 4¹⁵⁄₁₆" apart. I also cut router edges on the top of the base, except for the back.

It you choose to spray the final finish on the base, first glue the letters on. If using oil, put the oil on first. The dowels should be glued in last in either case.

Step 11: Making the letters. For lettering the base I chose a computer font called Comic Sans MS because of the slight irregularity in design of the letters. That hides any minor deviations in cutting them. The font size used was 36 point. I also chose to cut the letters from a ⅛"-thick strip of walnut ripped from a ¾" board.

The normal blade opening in the saw table is too large to cut these letters. The blade will catch the wood on the downstroke and rip part of the letter out of the wood. In order to avoid this, one needs a zero clearance throat plate (one with a very small blade hole) in the saw.

The letters were cut with a #1 reverse-tooth blade. Make the inside cuts of letters such as *o* before cutting the outside. Drill a blade entry hole alongside each letter, using it to access the letter rather than cutting to the letter from the edge of the wood. This allows the wood around the letter to give better support while it's being cut. During cutting, hold the letter down with one finger close to the blade so the blade will not lift the wood and split off a portion. If this does happen, it can usually be glued back on, but it will probably be even easier to cut a new letter. Remember that glue on the face of the letter can block stain you may want to use. Most types of glue can be removed with paint thinner if used before it completely dries.

After cutting the letters, remove the glue residue from the front of them with mineral spirits. Sand the front and back of each letter by rubbing it a few times across a piece of 400-grit sandpaper. Drop the finished letters into a pan of tung oil for a few minutes, then blot them before letting them dry. Repeat the process once.

▶ **Step 12: Attaching the letters.** Glue the letters to the base as you want them to look. To help line up the letters, clamp a strip of scrap wood to the base. Use it as a guideline against which the letters can be set. Clamping tweezers make manipulating the tiny letters easy. Attach a description of the wooly mammoth to the bottom of the base, if you'd like.

Step 13: Finishing the puzzle pieces. Assemble the puzzle and sand both the fronts and backs, finishing with 400-grit sandpaper. After vacuuming the sawdust, spray them using a minimum of three coats of polycrylic on front, back, and sides. A light rubbing with 0000 steel wool between each coat and a final light rub takes any roughness from adjoining edges. If the dowel holes become clogged, enlarge them slightly by wiggling them on the 1/8"-diameter drill bit.

For an oil finish, soak one sanded piece in a pan with tung oil for a few minutes, dunking it a few times. Put another piece in. Take the first piece out and blot it with a paper shop towel, using cotton-tipped swabs and the corners of the towel to blot all excess oil in tight nooks and crannies. Then rub thoroughly with a clean lint-free cloth. Set it back side down on a paper towel. Repeat with the next piece.

After each piece has been sitting for about five minutes, buff the top again. If you find any sticky places, rub until dry. If it is too sticky to buff off, apply more oil and rub to take the sticky spot off. Repeat for all pieces. After letting them dry for at least a day, repeat the oil application. Don't forget to sign and date your work.

Materials & Tools

Materials:
- 3 pieces, 1" x 3" x 14" poplar, edge-glued to form a ¾" x 8¼" x 14" board
- For a vertical grain pattern: 4 pieces, 1" x 4" x 8", edge-glued to form a ¾" x 8" x 15" board
- 1" x 3" x 11" poplar (base)
- 2 each 1/8"-diameter hardwood dowel cut into 1" segments
- 2 each 1/8" x ¾" x 6" ripped from a walnut board (lettering)
- Permanent marking pen
- Elmer's Glue-All
- Temporary spray glue or a removable glue stick
- Minwax ebony stain or wood stain of choice
- Wood glue
- Jeweler's glue, Bond 527
- Odorless paint thinner or mineral spirits
- Tung oil and/or polycrylic satin spray
- Sandpaper and 0000 steel wool
- Shop cloths, paper and fabric
- Cotton swabs

Tools:
- #1 reverse-tooth, #3, #4, and #5 double-tooth blades
- Drill press and bits
- Combination square or plastic triangles
- Small clamps
- Illuminated magnifying glass for cutting
- Clamping tweezers
- Handheld rotary tool and diamond-point grinders

To mount the mammoth as an upright puzzle, assemble the puzzle on a table then slide it onto a sheet of plywood or cardboard. Place the sheet on the table with the feet at the edge of both the sheet and table. Slide the base pegs into the holes in the feet. Tip the whole thing up with the sheet.

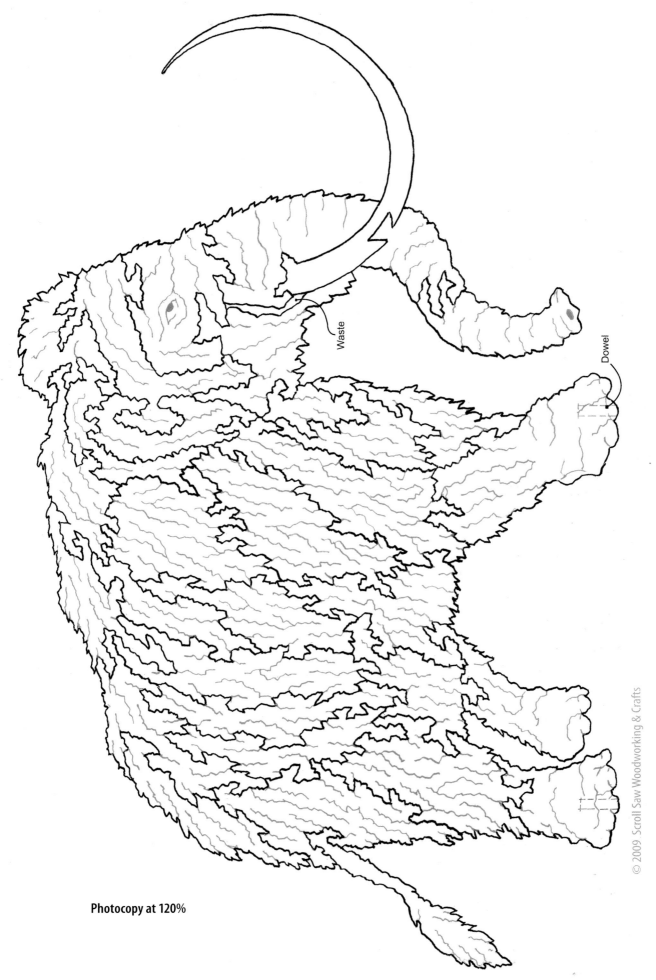

Waste

Dowel

Photocopy at 120%

© 2009 Scroll Saw Woodworking & Crafts

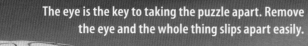

Lateral Locking Lizard Puzzle

Show off your skills with this unique, compound-cut puzzle

By Len Wardle

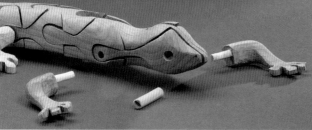

The eye is the key to taking the puzzle apart. Remove the eye and the whole thing slips apart easily.

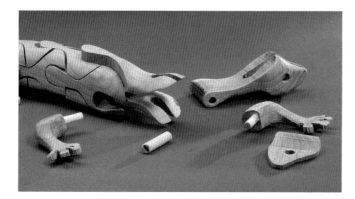

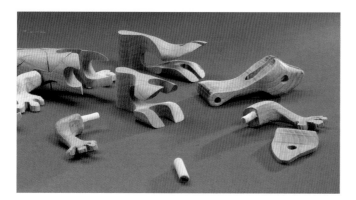

Normally, the fun of a puzzle is figuring out how to put it together. But, this puzzle is as fun to take apart as it is to put together. Part of the fun is that it doesn't come right apart—hand it to someone and watch them struggle to take it apart without breaking it.

Start by choosing the materials for the project. I use hardwood for all my puzzles—it's just more durable. Black cherry is very nice for the lizard; walnut is a close second. But use what you want. You can also choose to give the lizard a longer tail—just add a few inches to the tail right where it starts, but don't add any more to the taper.

After choosing your wood, transfer the pattern to the work piece. I trace the side and top views onto poster board or a similar material, cut it out and trace around these templates onto the wood. That way I can use the same template over and over again.

Step 1: Cut the basic shape of the lizard using your patterns as a guide. Cut along the top view pattern first, but leave about ⅛" of wood holding each piece on—so you still have square sides to rest on your scroll saw table, giving you accurate cuts. After you make the side cuts, it will be easy to go back and cut the small amount of wood holding the pieces on. After making the cuts, drill the leg and eye holes as indicated on the pattern.

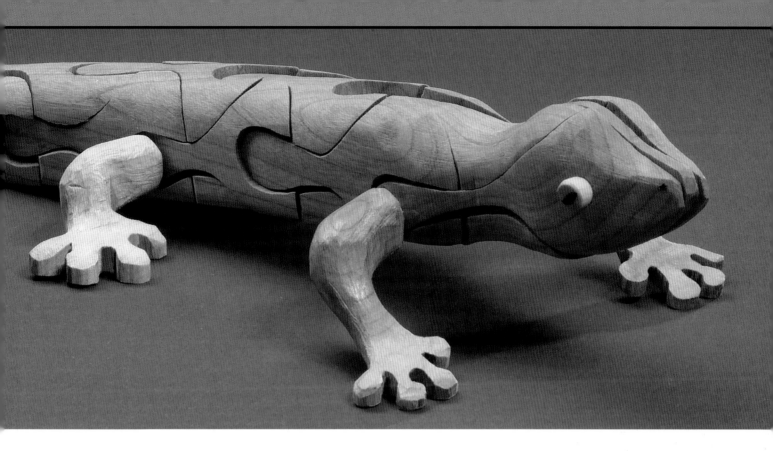

Step 2: Make the legs. Draw a top view of each leg on a 1½"-thick piece of wood. Then, cut out the side views to get two perfectly matching legs for the front and the back. Shape the legs lightly with fine sandpaper.

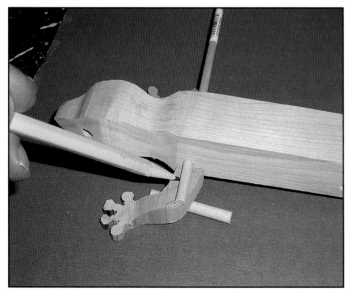

▲ **Step 3: Insert a dowel through the lizard body to determine the drilling angle for the legs.** Position the feet beside the dowel and draw a line on the foot along the dowel—this will give you the correct angle to drill the holes for the feet. Dry fit each dowel to make sure it fits properly (see *Check the Tightness of the Dowels* on page 95) before gluing the dowels to the legs.

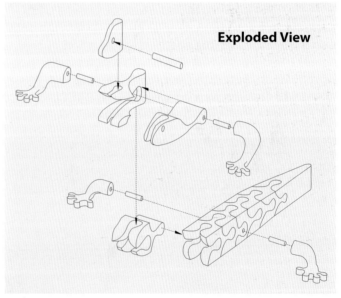

Exploded View

Once you remove the eye, the pieces of the lizard puzzle slide apart easily. Because the pieces actually lock together, you have to take the puzzle apart—and put it back together—in order.

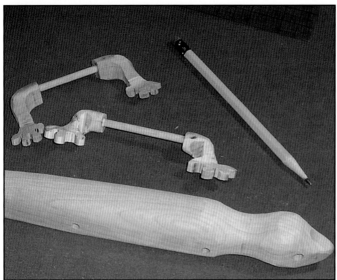

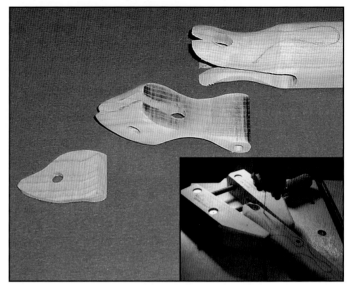

▲ Step 4: Round off the sharp corners of the lizard. Hold the head in your left hand and the tail section in your right hand. Place the top of the lizard on the belt sander, and "rock" the lizard to round off the sharp angle where the body tapers down to the tail. Round off this sharp angle on the top, left, and right sides. Rock the top of the lizard clockwise and counterclockwise to curve the top. Use the rounded part of the belt sander or a drum sander to smooth out the lizard's neck between the body and the head. Shape the head with a rotary tool and small sanding drum. Hand sand with progressively finer grits of sandpaper for the best finish. Alternatively, you can shape the head by hand sanding; it will just take a little longer.

▲ Step 6: Rotate the body 90°, and make the second cut. Try not to come too close to the leg holes when cutting; it just doesn't look good with a cut line right through the hole you put the leg in. Notice how each leg hole is in a large part of a puzzle piece. Take your time and let the blade cut at its own speed. When you try to rush, the blade will tend to wander.

Step 7: Continue to cut out the pieces, making sure to keep them in order. There are no puzzle cuts in the long tail; the tail is too thin and the pieces would be too delicate.

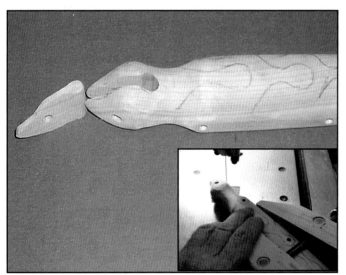

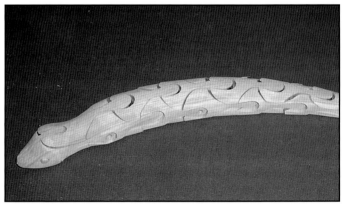

▲ Step 8: Assemble the lizard, and sand off the pencil marks and burrs. Cut a length of ³⁄₁₆"-diameter dowel for the eye. Lightly round off both sides of the dowel.

Step 9: Sand the puzzle with very fine (320-grit) sandpaper, and apply the finish of your choice. You can paint, woodburn, or just draw in the eye details with a pen or pencil. I gave my lizard a "cat eye."

▲ Step 5: Make the first puzzle cut. Start by transferring the puzzle-cutting pattern to the project. Use a wooden hand clamp to hold the body—so you can hold the lizard in place at a 90° angle to the saw table. If you don't keep the lizard body square to the table, you will cut into the holes for the legs! I just free handed the lines on, but you can trace the pattern using graphite paper.

Materials & Tools

Materials:

- 1½" x 1½" x 17" hardwood of choice (body)
- 2 pieces 1" x 2" x 3½" hardwood of choice (feet)
- ³⁄₁₆"-diameter dowel 12" long
- Various grits of sandpaper
- Oil finish of choice
- Black paint (optional)
- Graphite paper
- Wood glue

Tools:

- #9 skip-tooth blades or blades of choice
- Drill with ³⁄₁₆"-diameter drill bit
- Belt sander or drum sander
- Rotary tool with ½"-diameter and ¼"-diameter sanding drums (optional)
- Pencil
- Woodburner (optional for eye)
- Pen (optional for eye)
- Fine artist's brush (optional for eye)

Check the Tightness of the Dowels

Using a piece of scrap wood, drill holes the same diameter you plan to use in the lizard, and check the fit of the dowels. You want a tight fit, but if they are too tight, they could break when you try to remove them. After drilling the dowel holes in the legs, "dry fit" the drilled legs to the dowel, sanding the dowels if necessary to make them fit better.

If you do get a leg stuck, cut a very gradual wedge in a piece of soft wood. Then, cut a slot the same size as the dowel in the wedge. Line the slot up around the leg, and tap it lightly to pop the leg off (see photo below).

If you don't take the time to fit the dowel into the body properly, it's difficult to remove legs without breaking something.

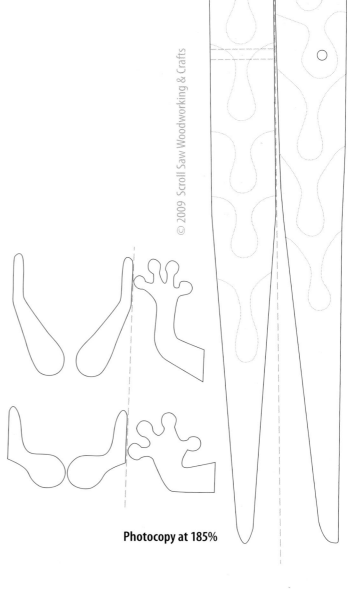

© 2009 Scroll Saw Woodworking & Crafts

Photocopy at 185%

Motorcycle Puzzles

Quick freestanding puzzles make great gifts

By William Berry

These motorcycles are inspired by the puzzles designed by Judy and Dave Peterson. They make great craft show items and I have a hard time keeping up with demand.

They can be cut from a number of woods, but due to the various angles, there will be fragile areas. I've cut them from padauk, bubinga, maple, oak, and poplar. I usually stain the poplar, but have had requests to paint them.

Attach the pattern to your blank and drill the blade entry holes for all interior cuts. For easy assembly, it is important to make sure your blade is square to the saw table.

Step 1: Cut the interior cuts and puzzle pieces. Start with the interior cuts, then cut each puzzle piece individually, moving from one end to the other. Rotate your work clockwise whenever possible. For a round tire with minimal tool marks, make one slow, continuous cut without stopping.

Step 2: Make the accent cuts. Cut any accent lines before freeing the piece from the rest of the board. It is easier to cut the details while you still have stock to hold onto.

Step 3: Sand the surface to remove any defects. Clean up the sides with a pad sander and round over the edges with a flap sander. You can also sand the entire project by hand; it will just take longer.

Step 4: Remove the sawdust from the pieces. Use compressed air, a vacuum, or a tack cloth.

Step 5: Apply a finish. For hardwoods, apply a coat of Danish oil according to the manufacturer's instructions. To stain the puzzle, dip the individual pieces into the stain. Wipe off the excess, and place on a paper towel to dry. When dry, apply a coat of polyurethane to protect the finish. For a simple paint job, apply the appropriate colors to each puzzle piece. I use metallic silver for any chrome parts. Paint over the edges of the pieces where the rounding ends, so no wood shows in between pieces when assembled. Apply a clear coat when dry.

Caution:
These puzzles contain small pieces which can be a potential choking hazard. This project is not intended for children under 3 years of age.

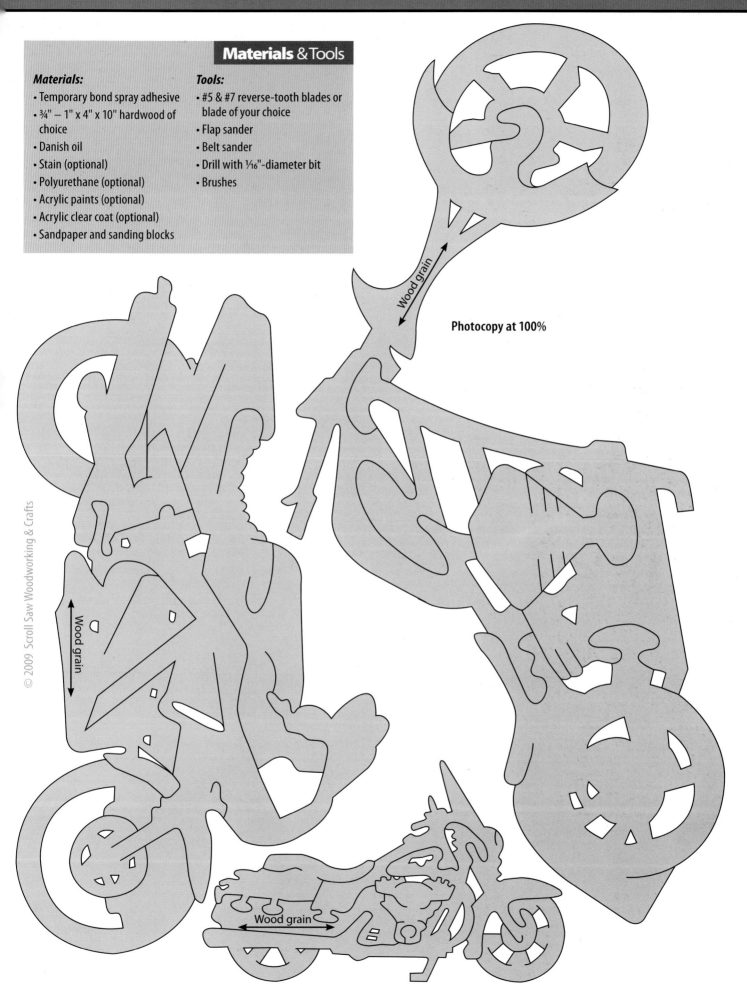

Materials & Tools

Materials:
- Temporary bond spray adhesive
- ¾" – 1" x 4" x 10" hardwood of choice
- Danish oil
- Stain (optional)
- Polyurethane (optional)
- Acrylic paints (optional)
- Acrylic clear coat (optional)
- Sandpaper and sanding blocks

Tools:
- #5 & #7 reverse-tooth blades or blade of your choice
- Flap sander
- Belt sander
- Drill with ¹⁄₁₆"-diameter bit
- Brushes

Wood grain

Photocopy at 100%

Wood grain

Wood grain

© 2009 Scroll Saw Woodworking & Crafts

Hidden Images Puzzle

Distinctly shaped pieces add character to this hand cut puzzle.

Match unusual shapes with your photo's theme for a unique and challenging puzzle

By Carl Hird-Rutter

I love a good jigsaw puzzle and am amazed at the talent of scrollers like Carter Johnson and Steve Malavolta, who are able to design interlocking pieces in their mind and cut them out freehand. These artists produce custom works of art that are highly valued.

Being a little less creative, I felt the need to design a pattern for my puzzle, which created a few challenges of its own. I needed to determine how to transfer my puzzle pattern to the work piece without damaging the puzzle's photo. I also needed to design a pattern that is simple enough to cut, but challenging enough for the scroller and the end user.

After experimenting with several designs, I decided to incorporate a puzzle within a puzzle. I chose a large silhouette of a duck to keep in theme with my photo and incorporated several smaller shapes both within the duck silhouette and outside of it.

Attaching the Pattern to the Blank

How do you attach a pattern and make it so you can remove it without damaging the picture? My first thought was to attach the pattern to the back of the puzzle. No one will know the pattern is backwards because the shapes have no front or back. As I cut, I noticed that the teeth of the saw were lifting the edges of the picture on the other side of the puzzle. It was a valiant attempt, but it fell flat. The finished puzzle had lifting edges on all of the pieces. Then I had to wrestle the pattern off the back of each piece.

The next process I tried was to attach the pattern overtop of the photo but only secure it at the edges. I used masking tape around the perimeter of the pattern, wrapped around to the back of the puzzle. By cutting the puzzle in strips, the pattern will remain attached to the outer edge of each strip. I then cut the pieces out from the strips starting from one edge and working to the other. I did have to hold the free end of the pattern down with my fingers.

Building off this method, I applied the pattern to a piece of extra stock and stacked the pattern piece on top of the puzzle with the photo using tape around the perimeter. I then used the strip method to cut the individual pieces. The extra stock can be discarded or you can assemble the pieces and have a child color their own custom jigsaw puzzle.

Step 1: Attach the color picture. You can use ⅛" or ¼"-thick Baltic birch plywood or MDF. I tried three different methods. Apply spray adhesive to both the wood and the paper. This only works if you get a generous coating on both; otherwise, the paper lifts on the edge of the pieces. Another method is to apply varathane to the wood; then put the paper down, and apply another coat of varathane over the paper. This may cause the paper to wrinkle slightly. The best solution was Modge Podge, a découpage glue. Apply the Modge Podge according to the manufacturer's directions.

A REAL CHALLENGE — TIP

For a diabolical twist, why not glue the picture to both sides of the wood before you cut out the puzzle!

Step 2: Attach the jigsaw pattern. Attach the pattern to the extra piece of stock and stack the pattern piece on top of the puzzle stock. Securely attach the two pieces with blue painter's tape. Be sure to tape around the entire perimeter.

Step 3: Cut the pattern into strips. Ensure that there is tape at both ends to hold the pattern in position. If you are cutting the tessellation pattern, it is best to cut each individual piece from the puzzle as you go along. Do NOT cut this puzzle in strips.

Step 4: Cut out the individual pieces. Take the first strip, and cut out the individual pieces starting at one end and working your way toward the opposite end. Place a piece of sandpaper on the bench, and touch up the underside of the pieces as you cut.

Step 5: Rebuild the puzzle as you go along. Put the completed puzzle in a box along with a small picture of the finished puzzle as a guide. You could make a nice wooden box with a sliding lid to create a unique gift suitable for anyone. You can even personalize the puzzle by choosing an alternate photo and altering the shapes to suit the photo's theme.

Materials & Tools

Materials:
- 2 pieces ¼" or ⅛" x 8" x 10½" Baltic birch plywood or MDF
- Spray adhesive
- Blue painters' tape
- Varathane or Modge Podge (optional)
- Assorted grits of sandpaper

Tools:
- #2/0 reverse-tooth blade or blade of choice
- Paintbrush to apply varathane or Modge Podge (optional)

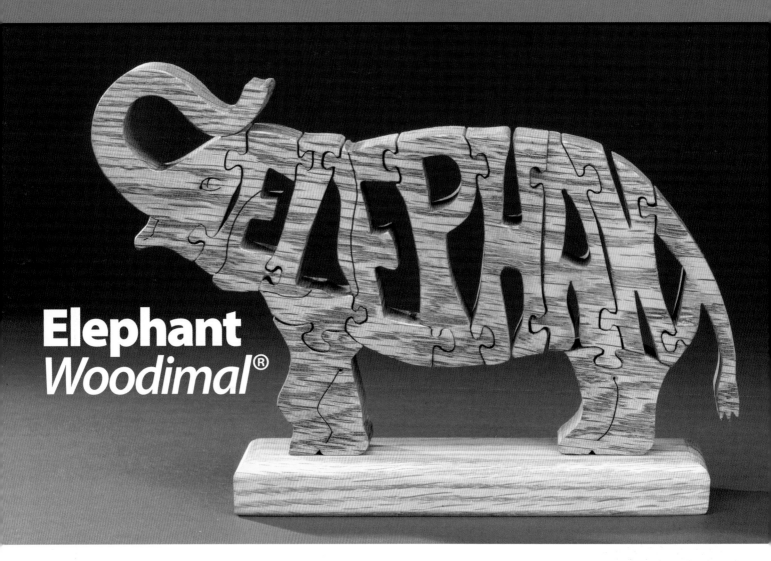

Elephant
Woodimal®

Scroll this clever puzzle that spells its own name

By James W. Sweet

The Elephant Woodimal is a fun design that is large enough for the youngest puzzle-assembler. Woodimals are whimsical little puzzles made up of letters that spell out the name of the animal they represent. What child (or adult) can resist a creative puzzle such as this? And the children won't even know they are learning something!

I use hardwoods to make my Woodimals, usually oak, ash, or poplar. On the pattern, the dotted lines are for painting reference only—DO NOT cut along those lines. If you are not comfortable scrolling the eyes, paint them on or burn them with a woodburner. Use a #5 reverse-tooth blade for most of the cutting, but use a #1 reverse-tooth blade for the veining details. I use a ⅛"-diameter drill bit for the blade entry holes for the letters and a #60 drill bit for the veining details.

After scrolling, mount the Elephant on a base. I round off the corners of the base with a ¼"-radius round-over router bit or a ¼"-radius ogee router bit. You can also round it over with sandpaper.

Materials & Tools

Materials:
- ¾" or ⅞" x 6" x 10" hardwood of choice (puzzle)
- ¾" x 2" x 8" matching hardwood of choice (base)
- Spray adhesive, transfer paper, carbon paper (to transfer pattern to work piece)
- Finish or paint of choice
- Assorted grits of sandpaper

Tools:
- #5 & #1 reverse-tooth tooth blades or blades of choice
- Drill with ⅛"-diameter and #60 drill bits
- Router with ¼"-radius round-over or ogee bit (optional)

Photocopy at 100%

Owl Family Puzzle

Scroll this freestanding puzzle for the animal lover in your life

By Judy and Dave Peterson

Scrolled hardwood animal puzzles are always a hit, both as gifts and at craft shows. The most difficult part of this puzzle is the eye details of the owlets' faces. Drill a blade entry hole for one eyeball, and then cut the "monkey face" of the owlets, starting in one eyehole.

Everyone cuts differently—Judy cuts to the right side of her blade (on the left side of the line)—so all of her patterns are set up to cut on the right side of the blade. When she started scrolling, she wasn't consistent about the position of the board and pattern, in relation to the scroll saw blade—and ended up with burnished surfaces. These burnished surfaces show up glossier than the surrounding areas after the puzzle is finished—so she spent a lot of time sanding the burnished areas off.

A presenter at a scroll-sawing demonstration suggested that she cut on the right side of the blade. Because of the way scroll saw blades are manufactured, the teeth end up canted to the right. To compensate for this, push the board into the blade so the teeth are tilted toward the line you are cutting. When you come to a turning point in the pattern, turn the board clockwise to keep the blade in the correct position with respect to the line you're cutting. If you cut on the left side of the blade, it is more likely to burnish the wood.

The Owl Family, designed and cut by Judy Peterson, is a popular puzzle at craft shows.

Materials & Tools

Materials:
- ⅞" x 8" x 8" hardwood of choice (I use spalted cherry)
- Repositionable spray adhesive
- Sandpaper, 220 grit
- Sanding disk

Tools:
- #9 skip-tooth or reverse-tooth blades or blades of choice
- Square
- Disk pad
- Drill with variable speed lock
- Drill stand
- Flap sander

Photocopy at 100%

SQUARING YOUR BLADE   **TIP**

Make sure your blade is square to your saw table. There are several ways to check for square, such as using a small square against the blade or cutting a piece of scrap and checking that for square. If your table and blade are not square when cutting a puzzle, it will be difficult to reassemble the completed puzzle.

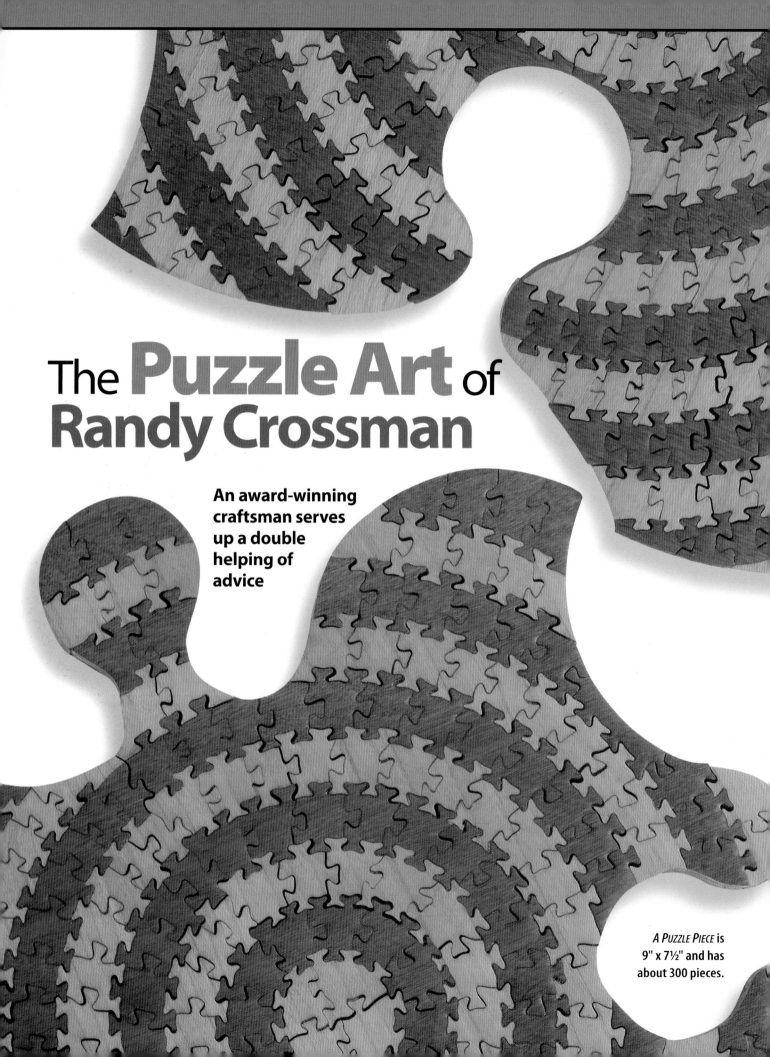

The **Puzzle Art** of **Randy Crossman**

An award-winning craftsman serves up a double helping of advice

A PUZZLE PIECE is 9" x 7½" and has about 300 pieces.

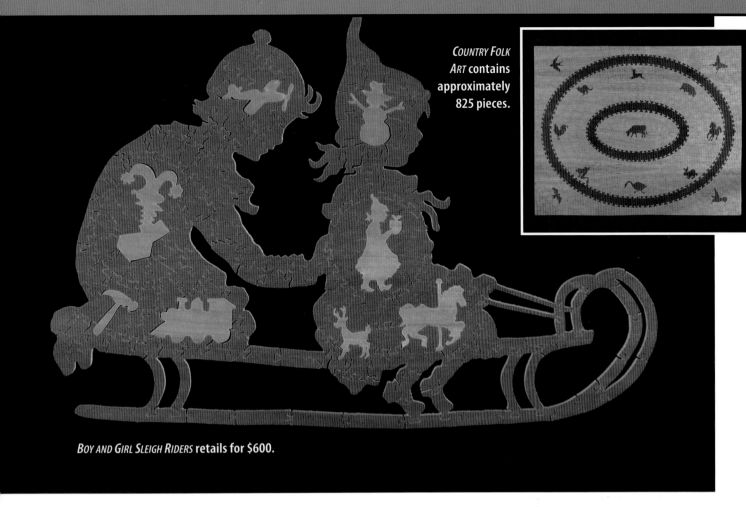

COUNTRY FOLK ART contains approximately 825 pieces.

BOY AND GIRL SLEIGH RIDERS retails for $600.

Learn how to cut freehand puzzles. And see how you can build a successful business based on your own creativity and original designs.

By Bob Duncan

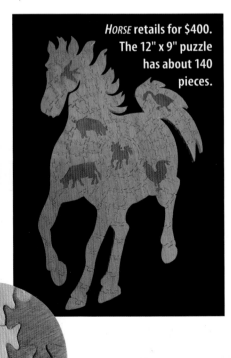

HORSE retails for $400. The 12" x 9" puzzle has about 140 pieces.

Twenty years ago, when Randy Crossman was a stay-at-home dad, he began cutting puzzles on the scroll saw in his spare time. It started out as a welcome diversion that ultimately garnered national exposure. Randy's puzzles now offer a way to supplement the income received from his custom furniture business.

Randy met his business partner, Bruce Marston, when looking for a location to practice his woodworking. The two men ended up renting the same property and quickly discovered they had more in common than a real estate lease. Both were highly accomplished craftsmen with a deep respect for traditional handmade methods. They were well versed in nineteenth century furniture styles and their love of old-fashioned sleighs led them to start a joint venture called the Vermont Sleigh Company.

The company produces decorative sleighs as well as custom furniture featuring the distinctive sleigh design. Randy began inlaying puzzles in the tabletops as a way to combine his hobby with his livelihood and soon realized there was a market for his custom puzzles.

The side business, now known as X-Man Puzzles, began with a few sales of his large puzzles. These puzzles average between 2,000 and 4,000 pieces and can take six to eight months to cut.

"I don't make a living with my puzzle business," Randy said. "When I set up the X-Man Puzzles Web site, I decided on a few rules for myself. I do the best work I can, and I do not compromise on anything. I set the prices for my high-end puzzles and don't negotiate that price just to make a sale. In the high-end market I'm trying to create, there is no one out there doing what I'm doing."

The hardest part about launching Randy's side business of custom puzzles was getting the word out. While he stresses the importance

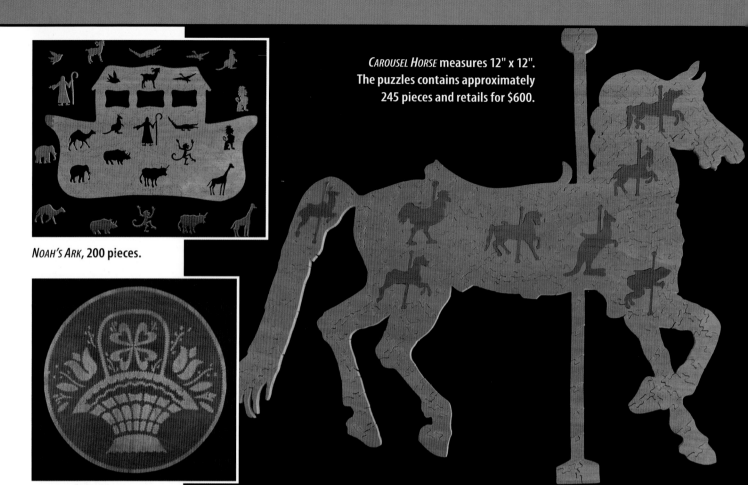

NOAH'S ARK, 200 pieces.

CAROUSEL HORSE measures 12" x 12". The puzzles contains approximately 245 pieces and retails for $600.

BASKET, over 4,000 pieces.

of creating an attractive Web site with really nice photos, and keeping that Web site updated, Randy found the best way to spread the word about his puzzles was through press releases.

"Take a unique and interesting item you have in your product line," he said. "You've got to have a good and unusual project. Something the magazine's readers would be interested in. Physically mail a press release to anyone who might have an interest in it. Don't e-mail something; most people delete e-mails like that. If you really want to make an impression on a publisher or an editor, do the groundwork and call ahead to see what person specifically to send the release to."

The technique works. Randy has had his work featured in nearly 20 publications including *Better Homes and Gardens, Sleigh Magazine,* and *Southern Living,* earning him national recognition.

Like most scrollers, Randy struggles with pricing his work. It can take a bit of trial and error to find out what the market will bear. "People have to decide if they want to sell their pieces themselves or through a gallery," he said. "You can't price it both ways. If you find a retail price where your product sells, in order to sell that through a gallery, you need to be willing to accept 40% less. But if you are marketing your product directly to the public, it takes time, money, and patience to build up a clientele, which you get automatically by selling through a gallery."

Due to the labor involved with his large puzzles, Randy realizes that if he wants to get paid for his time, his pricing structure will produce a limited customer base. He continues to create them because he loves doing it and wants to share his work with the public. To increase the profitability of X-Man Puzzles, Randy has started designing a lower-end puzzle line. This new line features puzzles cut from business cards as well as folk-style puzzles small enough to fit into a CD case. He continues to use his scrolling skills to embellish custom furniture and is always on the look out for new ways to expand his business.

Randy strongly believes there will always be a demand for handcrafted, high-quality goods and is thankful his skills and talent allow him to serve that market.

Cutting a Puzzle Freehand

By Randy Crossman

My puzzle patterns start with an original line drawing that I break down into sections. These sections help to keep things symmetrical. Each individual puzzle piece is cut freehand inside the sections.

I use three-ply, ¼"-thick cherry plywood. I stack two pieces together with double-sided masking tape. One piece is left the natural color of the wood. The other piece is either rotated 90°, so the grain is in the opposite direction, darkened with a dark cherry stain, or both. That way I can mix and match pieces to give each puzzle a unique look. It is very important to have your saw table square to the blade when cutting puzzles, otherwise the pieces won't fit together easily.

In the steps below, I'll demonstrate my freehand cutting technique. For those hesitant to give this technique a try, I've included a pattern for my Folk Art Snowman that can be gift boxed in a CD case.

1 **Prepare the pattern.** Start with a simple line drawing and use a compass to draw concentric circles to guide your cuts. Adhere the pattern to the blank, using your method of choice. Attach the two blanks together with double-sided masking tape. Rotate one piece 90° so the grain runs in opposite directions between the two pieces.

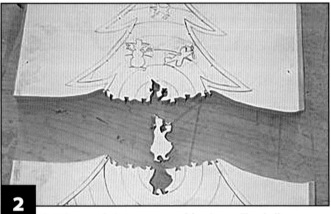

2 **Cut the puzzle into manageable pieces.** The challenge is to cut it into sections so the sectioning cut is disguised among the other puzzle cuts. You don't want the line to be obvious. Remember to cut lobes inside each ring or section of the puzzle.

3 **Cut out the concentric rings and internal images.** Use the circles as a guide, but cut out the lobes and sockets freehand. Do not worry about cutting out the individual pieces right now; continue breaking the puzzle into more manageable pieces.

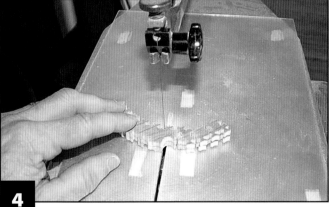

4 **Cut out the puzzle pieces.** Each ring is broken down into individual pieces. Vary the position of the lobe and socket to add interest. I use a piece of clear acrylic as a zero-clearance insert.

5 **Separate the stacks.** Sand off any rough edges left by the cutting process. Assemble the puzzles and place them side-by-side to decide which pieces to mix and match.

6 **Stain the pieces for contrast.** I like to set off the shaped pieces by using a dark cherry spray stain. For this project, I also use a green marker to color in the frame of the puzzle.

7 **Finish the puzzle.** Apply a coat of clear lacquer to the entire puzzle. Take a photo of the completed puzzle and include it to aid the new owner in assembly.

Materials & Tools

Materials:
- 2 pieces ¼" x 4" x 4½" three-ply cherry plywood or plywood of choice
- Cherry spray stain
- Assorted grits of sandpaper
- Double-sided masking tape
- Spray lacquer
- Spray adhesive
- Clear acrylic or zero-clearance insert material of choice

Tools:
- #0, #1, or #2 Eberle double-tooth blades or blades of choice

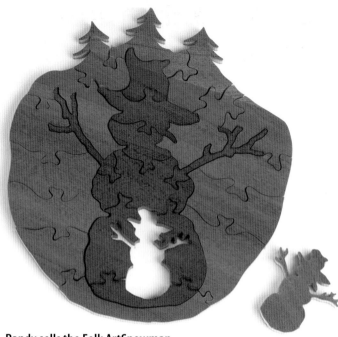

Randy sells the Folk Art Snowman puzzle, which has 24 pieces, for $46.

Photocopy at 100%

List of Contributors

William Berry
William Berry's scrolling business is based in Saline, MI.
www.taurpiocreations.com

Bob Betting
Bob Betting, a Colorado native, invented Paleo Pets puzzles.

Charles Bowman
Charles, resident of Kentwood, MI, is also an electronics technician, professional magician, certified hypnotist, and writer.

Randy Crossman
Randy lives in Rutland, VT, where he co-operates Yankee Woodworking, Vermont Sleigh Company, Trailsigns.net, and X-Man Puzzles.
www.xmanpuzzles.com

Russell Greenslade
Russell Greenslade, of Girard, OH, sells his unique puzzles through art galleries and craft shows.

Carl Hird-Rutter
Carl lives in British Columbia, Canada.
www3.telus.net/public/scroller/

Donald Horgan
Donald lives in Antioch, CA. He is a self-taught woodworker.

Joanne Lockwood
Joanne Lockwood has been teaching scroll sawing for more than 15 years. She lives in Sparks, NV.

Steve Malavolta
Steve lives and works in Albuquerque, NM. He sells kits for many of his puzzle designs.
Escapader@aol.com

John Morgan
When he's not scrolling, John enjoys playing his trumpet, spending time with his family, and cooking.
www.woodjam.com

John A. Nelson
John, a prolific scroller and designer, contributes frequently to *Scroll Saw Woodworking & Crafts*.
www.scrollsawer.com

Judy and Dave Peterson
Judy and Dave live in Wisconsin. Judy makes the puzzles and Dave runs the business side. They've published several puzzle books with Fox Chapel Publishing.

Jim Sonnleitner
Jim, a pilot and full-blown airplane nut, lives in Wisconsin.

Jim Stirling
Australian-born Jim is known for using his unique relief techniques to scroll collapsible castles. He lives in Norway.
www.stirling.no

James W. Sweet
James took up woodcrafts when he retired in 1989 from a 40-year career in the aerospace industry.
www.woodimals.com

Len Wardle
Len has designed many puzzles, including reptiles, fish, dolphins, and more.
www.members.cox.net/lvpuzzle

Tom Zieg
Tom loves to share his knowledge of woodworking with others.
www.woodworkertom.com

Index

More Great Project Books from Fox Chapel Publishing

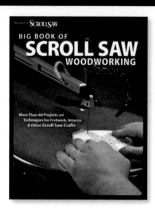

Big Book of Scroll Saw Woodworking
More Than 60 Projects and Techniques for Fretwork, Intarsia & Other Scroll Saw Crafts
By Editors of *Scroll Saw Woodworking & Crafts*

From the Best of *Scroll Saw Woodworking & Crafts* comes a collection of the most popular projects and useful scrolling techniques perfect for crafters of all skill levels.

ISBN: 978-1-56523-426-0
$24.95 • 192 Pages

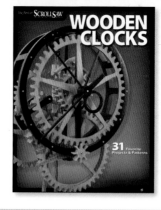

Wooden Clocks
By Editors of *Scroll Saw Woodworking & Crafts*

The most beloved clock projects from the pages of *Scroll Saw Woodworking & Crafts*. Includes grandfather clocks, pendulum clocks, desk clocks, and more.

ISBN: 978-1-56523-427-7
$24.95 • 152 Pages

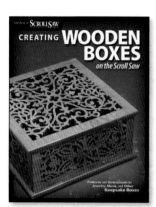

Creating Wooden Boxes on the Scroll Saw
Patterns and Instructions for Jewelry, Music, and Other Keepsake Boxes
By Editors of *Scroll Saw Woodworking & Crafts*

Includes more than 20 projects for making a variety of boxes with your scroll saw: music boxes, memory boxes, and more.

ISBN: 978-1-56523-444-4
$19.95 • 128 Pages

Animal Puzzles for the Scroll Saw—2nd Edition
By Judy & Dave Peterson

Newly expanded to include 20 fresh new animal puzzle patterns! Step-by-step instructions for making Mama Rabbit with Babies along with 50 great patterns.

ISBN: 978-1-56523-391-1
$17.95 • 128 Pages

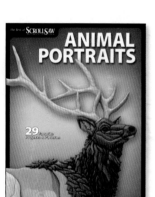

Animal Portraits
29 Favorite Projects & Patterns
By Editors of *Scroll Saw Woodworking & Crafts*

Join your favorite authors from *Scroll Saw Woodworking & Crafts* as they scroll extraordinary projects from the animal kingdom.

ISBN: 978-1-56523-502-1
$19.95 • 128 Pages

Zodiac Puzzles for Scroll Saw Woodworking
By Judy & Dave Peterson

Crafters will find inspiration in the stars with this collection of scroll saw patterns based on the astrological signs of the Western and Eastern zodiacs.

ISBN: 978-1-56523-393-5
$17.95 • 96 Pages

Fantasy & Legend Scroll Saw Puzzles
By Judy & Dave Peterson

29 easy-to-follow instructions for puzzles depicting fabled creatures from Greek mythology and other storied traditions.

ISBN: 978-1-56523-256-3
$14.95 • 80 Pages

SCROLLSAW
Woodworking & Crafts

In addition to being a leading source of woodworking books and DVDs, Fox Chapel also publishes *Scroll Saw Woodworking & Crafts*. Released quarterly, it delivers premium projects, expert tips and techniques from today's finest woodworking artists, and in-depth information about the latest tools, equipment, and materials.

Subscribe Today!
Scroll Saw Woodworking & Crafts: **888-840-8590**
www.FoxChapelPublishing.com